Developing Global Talent
~Competing against the best in the world~

Ikuko Atsumi

Copyright © 2017 by Ikuko Atsumi

Developing Global Talent
~Competing against the best in the world~

Translated by Mandi Haase.
Translation supervised by Laura Cocora
Coordinator: Junko Rodriguez
Formatting: Sota Torigoe

Published by Babel Press U.S.A.
All rights reserved

ISBN: 978-0991478910

Babel Corporation
Pacific Business News Bldg. #208,
1833 Kalakaua Avenue, Honolulu, Hawaii 96815

INTRODUCTION

There is a haze enshrouding the whole country ....

At least that was how I felt when, in the summer of 2007, I returned to Japan after living abroad for 25 years. What enveloped Japan was not a haze of smog, but a haze of *information.*

At a time when globalization was transforming values and structures around the world at a relentless pace, the Japanese appeared oblivious to its impacts.

Wondering what was going on, I decided to explore further and embarked on a series of meetings with various experts, ranging from managers from major corporations, to media professionals and scholars. To my surprise, almost none of them seemed to have a clear grasp of the real significance of globalization.

I visited Japanese megabanks advertising themselves as "global routes," only to find that their internal organization was a far cry from being "globalized." One executive of a leading newspaper that routinely stressed the importance of globalization laughed as he commented, "As for us, we are *super* domestic."

Sure enough, most of the presidents of major corporations whom I met with had a clear understanding of what globalization entailed. Nevertheless, expecting these corporate leaders to take the lead in Japan's push towards globalization at this late stage in the game was unrealistic.

Why had Japan missed the wave of globalization? One reason was that the fall of the Soviet Union, which ushered in a new era of globalization, occurred almost simultaneously with the collapse of Japan's bubble economy. As they turned within to address the mounting problems at home, the Japanese failed to engage with the massive upheaval that was transforming the world around them.

Returning to Japan, I was astounded to discover that a great deal of crucial information was not being conveyed domestically. Few media sources reported the true impact of phenomena such as the Internet or trade regulations. For instance, even as businesses worldwide were shifting away from the kaizen management approach and toward standards developed by the International Organization for Standardization (ISO), the Japanese continued to regard kaizen capability as a company's greatest asset and assumed it remained the global standard.

Information that had been circulating in the international arena for decades was presented in Japan as the most up-to-date. Problematic systems that had already become the object of risk management in the US continued to be imported into Japan unquestioned. Japan was struggling to stay afloat in the murky waters of "information chaos".

Fortunately, I lived in Canada and then the US in my early years, during Japan's struggle with the aftermath of its collapsed bubble economy. This enabled me to witness firsthand the impacts of globalization from "the outside".

While in the US, I set up a pioneering consultancy in personnel training.

INTRODUCTION

As a female Japanese entrepreneur, a rarity at the time, my business gained popularity and attracted clients from large, well-known corporations. Not only was I active in business training, but also in youth education.

Managing talent development for large corporations with operations on a global scale, I learned to respond quickly to the trends of globalization. This helped me gain recognition as an authority in global education in the US, while my firm benefited from the support of numerous corporations.

I returned to Japan determined to share the experience and knowhow I had acquired at the forefront of global education. But I soon found myself at a loss, daunted by the enormity of the task, unsure where to start.

I could set up an incorporated association. Or offer on-site global business training programs for corporate clients. I could lecture. Or train global education instructors for junior and high schools… While all of these ventures sounded good, they were easier said than done.

One problem was that, having lived abroad for so many years, I found it difficult to get my ideas across in Japan. I had become so accustomed to communicating in English, that my Japanese skills may have temporarily deteriorated. The bigger problem however stemmed from the information gap between Japan and other countries. People did not fully comprehend the true meaning of globalization. I was particularly shocked when someone I was working with suggested that globalization was "nothing more than megalomania." For those who do not live facing the world as a whole, the processes of globalization that are reshaping the world appear as mere delusions of grandeur.

Still, I was confident that in the next five years globalization would start to receive its due attention in Japan. Around 2010, a few large corporations actually began to focus on globalizing their activities. The Japanese government took measures to support global personnel training programs, giving rise to what might be called a "global boom" in Japan. The people, media, companies and schools who, until not long ago, had been indifferent to globalization, began calling out for the need to globalize.

While at first glance this appeared to be what I had hoped for, my uneasiness remained. I realized that what Japanese people called "globalization" was nothing more than an ineffective substitute.

Let us briefly touch upon the main problems underlying the misdirected view of globalization that became prevalent in Japan, which we will explore in more detail later in this book. First, consider the following terms: *international model* and *global model*. Not only are they different, but they are actually based on opposite perspectives and ideas. A conception of globalization grounded in the wrong perspectives and ideas can actually result in more harm than good.

An international model consists of relationships among individual countries. On the other hand, the term *global* - as indicated by the root word "globe" – demands a worldwide perspective. In reality, globalization as it is taking shape in Japan is no more than internationalization, or focusing on an international model.

One might ask, which country then portrays a correct global model? It is this type of question that is fundamentally misguided. An important guiding principle for the new era is to break free from "emulating" what may work for other countries, falsely assuming that a particular global model is ideal simply because it is used elsewhere.

Relying on an international model to promote globalization leads to nothing more than efforts to develop English language skills, purposefully employ foreign nationals, or perhaps send staff abroad. While all these efforts are meaningful, errors in any of these areas may actually result in seriously weakening Japan's global competitiveness.

I believe that in a global age, people should be judged by their ability, regardless of their ethnic background. As someone who is Japanese, it is my fervent hope to see Japan and its citizens playing an active role in the global community. In order to do so, Japanese people must structure their thinking around two pillars: valuing their *Japanese cultural DNA* and *sharing world values*.

Today, Japan still possesses remarkably rich traditions and technologies. Provided that the Japanese are able to transition to a mindset in tune with global trends, (rather than with the misguided assumptions that the Japanese may entertain about globalization), and to develop learning methods that stay one step ahead of the times, I trust that Japan will once more become a preeminent global player.

Ikuko Atsumi, 2013

....

TABLE OF CONTENTS

INTRODUCTION ... 6

CHAPTER 1
SUCCEEDING IN THE UNITED STATES AS A JAPANESE FEMALE ENTREPRENEUR ... 18

SEARCHING FOR A PLACE THAT WOULD BECOME MY HAVEN......18
THE TRAINING THAT CHANGED MY LIFE............20
PEERING THROUGH CULTURAL GLASSES.......23
STARTING UP A BUSINESS IS NO WALK IN THE PARK……..24
FEATURED IN TIME MAGAZINE………26
THE EMERGENCE OF COMPETITION: MOVING ON TO THE NEXT STAGE………28

CHAPTER 2
THE ENCOUNTER WITH GLOBALIZATION, AND ITS TRANSFORMATIVE IMPACT ... 30

"HAVE YOU READ THE GLOBALIZATION ARTICLE?".......30
A DRASTICALLY CHANGING WORLD………31
THE EMERGING WORLD MARKET AND THE CREATION OF A NEW BUSINESS MODEL………33
AN EYE-OPENING EXPERIENCE OF DIVERSITY AT IBM……35
TRAVELLING AROUND THE WORLD WITH THE NCR PROJECT………37
JAPANESE AND AMERICAN NOTIONS OF TEAMWORK ARE

PROFOUNDLY DIFFERENT......38
AN IBM EXECUTIVE APOLOGIZES.....39
FORD CORPORATION'S STRONG SENSE OF PRIDE...........41

CHAPTER 3
THE WORLD REVEALS ITSELF IN THE CULTURE FACTOR ... 42

KEY INFORMATION FOR GLOBAL SUCCESS?........42
WORKING TOGETHER WITH INSTRUCTORS FROM AROUND THE WORLD.......44
THE DIFFICULT BIRTH OF THE CULTURAL WORLD MAP.........45
DO ASIA AND SOUTH AMERICA SHARE A SIMILAR SENSE OF VALUES?........46
OUR DIFFERENCES ARE THE PRODUCT OF WHAT WE CONSIDER OUR CORE VALUES!.......48
TRACING HISTORY THROUGH THE EYES OF CHILDREN TO CREATE A COMMON WORLDWIDE EDUCATIONAL PROGRAM...........50
THREE ATTRIBUTES OF INFLUENTIAL GLOBAL LEADERS......53

CHAPTER 4
UNDERSTANDING THE TRUE MEANING OF GLOBALIZATION ... 56

WHAT IS GLOBALIZATION?........56
JAPAN'S FAILURE TO EMBRACE A GLOBAL MODEL........58
"EVERYTHING CHANGES".........61
A SHIFT IN THOUGHT PATTERNS: USING A MATRIX........64
TWENTY-TWO YEARS AGO, BARNEVIK WAS RIGHT ABOUT

GLOBALIZATION....72
THE IMPORTANCE OF MATRIX THINKING......73
THE JAPANESE MISUNDERSTANDING OF WHAT CONSTITUTES GLOBAL TALENT.......75

CHAPTER 5
CULTIVATING A GLOBAL MIND (THE FIRST PATH) ... 78

SOME MISTAKEN ASSUMPTIONS, BIG AND SMALL..........78
WHILE THE WORLD MOVES FORWARD, JAPAN IS HEADING IN THE OPPOSITE DIRECTION......79
FIVE PATHS TO BECOMING A TRUE GLOBAL PROFESSIONAL.....82
THE MOST FUNDAMENTAL THING OF ALL: HAVING A GLOBAL MIND.......83
USING THE MIND'S EYE.....84
SEVEN THOUGHT PATTERNS FOR BEING GLOBALLY COMPETITIVE....85

CHAPTER 6
A BIRD'S EYE VIEW: THE CULTURAL WORLD MAP (THE SECOND PATH) ... 100

THE CULTURAL WORLD MAP – AN ORIGINAL TOOL FOR SHAPING A CAPACIOUS VESSEL FOR THE MIND....100
CULTURAL OLYMPICS......101
CLASSIFYING THE WORLD INTO FOUR BROAD CULTURAL CODES....103
WHAT CAUSED THE TOYOTA RECALL CRISIS?......113

IN BRUNEI, WORK ADHERES TO A DIFFERENT SENSE OF TIME …..115
GUIDED BY THE GLOBAL NAVIGATOR………116
CULTURAL MOTIVATORS (SM) AND DEMOTIVATORS (SM)………121
FILLING IN THE BLANKS ON THE MENTAL MAP……..124
THREE PROBLEMS THE JAPANESE NEED TO SOLVE…..124
SCRAPBOOKING…..129

CHAPTER 7
ETHICS AND THE LEGAL MIND (THE THIRD PATH) ... 132

THE JAPANESE AND THE MORAL CODE…….132
ETHICS VERSUS MORALITY…..133
A LACK OF LEGAL AWARENESS…….134
RECOGNIZING THE RULE OF LAW AS ABSOLUTE…….136
THE LOCALS ARE ATTENTIVE OBSERVERS…..137
UNDERSTANDING THE WORLD'S PERSPECTIVES ON INTERNATIONAL INCIDENTS…..138
PROBLEMS ARISING FROM AN ABSENCE OF LEGAL AWARENESS……..139
LEARNING FROM OTHERS' MISTAKES…..141
BALANCING CULTURAL CODES……142

CHAPTER 8
REFINING JAPANESE CULTURAL DNA TO NURTURE JAPANESE-STYLE GLOBAL TALENT (THE FOURTH PATH) ... 144

JAPANESE CULTURAL DNA……144
WHY DID JAPAN BECOME A MANUFACTURING POWER?…….145

FROM MONOTHEISM TO SHINTOISM……….147
JAPANESE TRADITIONS AND FIVE CULTURE-SPECIFIC VALUES …….148
PRESENTING THREE IDENTITIES TO THE WORLD……153
THE TRUE MEANING OF SINCERITY……….156
TACIT COMMUNICATION DOES NOT WORK……158
APPRECIATING JAPAN'S UNKNOWN INNOVATION…..159
A NEW BUSINES MODEL THAT CAN MAKE A DIFFERENCE…..160

CHAPTER 9
A LEARNING APPROACH FOR THE TWENTY-FIRST CENTURY (THE FIFTH PATH) ... 164

THE FOUR STEPS OF A LEARNING APPROACH FOR THE TWENTY-FIRST CENTURY……164
THE MINDSETS OF PREDOMINANT ETHNIC GROUPS…..170
THE CHINESE (HAN) MINDSET…….171
THE TRICK TO LEARNING ENGLISH AND OTHER FOREIGN LANGUAGES……174
HOW TO TRAIN YOUR BRAIN TO CREATE NEXT GENERATION MODELS…..176

CONCLUSION ... 180

GLOSSARY OF TERMS ... 185
APPENDIX ... 189
REFERENCES ... 212
IKUKO ATSUMI PROFILE ... 213

CHAPTER 1
SUCCEEDING IN THE UNITED STATES AS A JAPANESE FEMALE ENTREPRENEUR
As a Pioneer in Cross-cultural Management Training

SEARCHING FOR A PLACE THAT WOULD BECOME MY HAVEN

In September of 1983, I purchased a home in the suburbs of Stow, Boston, and started up a cross-cultural management training company. It was here that I would dive into the world of global business.

How did I, a woman born and bred in Japan, the daughter of a bureaucrat father and a mother who worked as a university professor, come to start up a business in the United States? Let me begin with that story.

My particular journey from Japan to entrepreneurship in the United States is nested within a broader shift: the world's transition from the age of internationalization to the age of globalization. Understanding this shift makes it easier to see why the Japanese take on globalization was flawed.

Growing up, I had a difficult time finding a place to belong, a place where I would feel entirely at peace. I did not feel at home in Nagoya, my hometown, so I ventured to Tokyo in my third year in high school. After graduating from college, I no longer felt comfortable living in Japan, and decided to try out Canada, England, and finally the US.

My discomfort in Japan stemmed from the attitudes surrounding women at the time. My mother, a university professor, constantly complained that female professors had to work three times as hard as their male counterparts to gain recognition. I enjoyed studying likely because of my mother's influence, but never forgot what I was told in grade school: "you're so good in school you have a great chance of marrying a lawyer."

My father, on the other hand, was a high-ranking official in the municipal government. He was wined and dined at traditional high-end restaurants what seemed like almost every week. My mother found this unfair. Nagoya is a provincial town and so tended to be more stifling and old-fashioned, which made the contrast between my mother's and father's professional lives even more stark.

When I settled in Tokyo and later graduated from college, many large corporations were in their heyday of prosperity. Unfortunately, I had two strikes against me: I was a woman and my parents were divorced. This made finding employment at a large bank or corporation difficult, if not impossible.

With job hunting at a dead end, I decided instead to take the graduate school route. There I joined the English Literary Society of Japan, only to become even more disillusioned as I observed professors who worshipped English literature so unconditionally that they seemed to have lost their Japanese soul. After completing my studies, I moved to Canada to do research at the University of British Columbia and the University of Toronto. But even in Canada, it was clear to me that I was just passing through.

Later, I became a full-time lecturer at Aoyama Gakuin University, which allowed me to spend a summer at Cambridge University in England. Here, I could not see myself getting used to the strong sense of class consciousness that prevailed in British society.

Still, there must be a place other than Japan that would make my heart dance with joy and excitement. With that thought in mind, I began studying, one after another, religions and philosophies from around the world.

THE TRAINING THAT CHANGED MY LIFE

I returned to Japan and a job as associate professor at Aoyama Gakuin University, where I continued to do research while pursuing an interest in business. I worked with a print shop to publish a women's magazine, for which I also handled advertising. On several occasions, my lifestyle was featured in the media as a new model for women in Japan.

In spite of this professional success, my discomfort living in Japan was becoming unbearable. It was at this point that I was awarded a grant from an academic society in New York to conduct research in the US. I jumped at the chance with the intention of devoting myself wholeheartedly to my research activities.

In September of 1980, I began work on a new research project at Harvard University's Bunting Institute (now the Radcliffe Institute for Advanced Studies). The institute's atmosphere reminded me of my time at Newnham College in Cambridge. We even had the same tradition: on Friday afternoons, women fellows from the US and abroad would get together at a local pub to discuss our research and our experiences of cultural difference over a glass of sherry.

My research at Bunting focused on the "global transmission of culture."

I wanted to understand how values specific to a certain country or region spread to other countries and regions, producing impacts and leading to the development of new art forms and business models.

What I experienced next changed my life.

At the time, there was a highly popular experiential training program in the US called "The Forum". The program was by no means inexpensive and required long, grueling hours of training, but was widely acclaimed for its effectiveness at healing broken family relationships and helping couples build long-lasting marriages. The training was said to have a transformative effect on the participants, instilling in them a total commitment to follow through on their promises, and to express themselves fully, without worrying about what others thought. It was a "training arena" for mending human relationships.

I gave in to my friend's pressure and applied to participate in a session in Boston. The session cost about $1350 in today's dollars. At the beginning of the training, the instructor told participants to remove all accessories, including glasses, watches, and rings. We were also instructed to put away any alarms, cameras, and bags in a safe place. I resented being ordered around like that, to the point where I felt anger welling up within me, wondering what in the world the meaning of this seminar was. If I hadn't paid the money I did, I probably would have kicked the chair aside and left. This was precisely what the organizers were anticipating.

The seminar was as intense as rumors had reported. In one exercise participants had to stand alone on stage and stare into the eyes of someone in the audience for three minutes. Some found this so difficult that they started to shake uncontrollably and then collapsed on the ground from the effort.

In yet another exercise, we were asked to close our eyes, and one by one we shared our most horrifying experiences. To my surprise, one participant, an African American man well over 6 feet tall, suddenly burst into tears. "I am scared out of my mind when I have to walk alone down dark streets at night. When the police see who they think is a black person, they'll start shooting the first chance they get. My buddy was shot like that for no reason," the man sobbed.

Other participants also began confessing their fears, until sounds of suppressed crying filled the hall. I too could feel tears streaming down my face as I realized how self-centered I had been all this time in my perception of others, failing to notice our shared vulnerability.

"The Forum" integrated a diverse mix of "sciences of the mind," from Zen and other traditions of Eastern thought to contemporary European psychology.

After the training, I felt the hardened places in my heart soften. This experience played a significant part in my decision to leave my job, along with the status, mindset and connections that came with it, and begin anew in America. The discovery that a seminar could have life-altering effects nurtured my faith in the tremendous potential of taking teaching to a whole new level. This realization was a driving force in my future ventures.

PEERING THROUGH CULTURAL GLASSES

A couple of months before I finished my two years of research at Harvard, I received a request from an English language school located in the suburbs of Boston. "An executive from a major corporation is being transferred to Tokyo as president of their Japanese branch office. Would you be able to provide special training for him?" The appointee was the vice president of a well-known film manufacturing company. He would also be accompanied to Japan by an accountant from India.

From that moment on, I had numerous opportunities to speak with directors from venture firms and other large corporations located in Boston's "Route 128" area, where high-tech industries were concentrated at the time.

What surprised me in my conversations with these directors was how US-centric their attitudes and assumptions were. Even when travelling overseas for business, they took the universality of their own ways of doing things for granted, and would often complain after returning that "people there just don't get it."

It is perhaps unavoidable for anyone, no matter what country they are from, to bring into business a tendency to be ethnocentric – a way of thinking that revolves around their own country. However, being *this* domestically focused posed a problem. I pondered what the reason for this situation could be. The answer that I arrived at was "culture".

At the time, bringing the concept of "culture" into the world of business was rare. The word "culture" evoked images of cuisine and fashion, or, in the case of Japan, the tea ceremony or kabuki theater. Business, the "real deal" of pursuing profit, stood worlds apart from the light-hearted entertainment of culture.

But this partitioning of culture from business is arbitrary. I came to the conclusion that we all need to become conscious of our own "cultural glasses": the "cultural glasses" through which we look will determine the outcome of how we perceive the world. Differences in culture cause management styles to vary even from one capitalist society to another. It is therefore impossible to conduct business on a global scale without appreciating cultural diversity and its influence on management styles.

It was at this point that I made up my mind to found a training company that would teach the cross-cultural management skills that these American corporate executives were lacking. It was ten years before the demise of the Soviet Union and the arrival of globalization in full force.

STARTING UP A BUSINESS IS NO WALK IN THE PARK

In September of 1983 I sold my property in Tokyo and purchased a brand-new, beautiful residence built on what had formerly been an apple orchard on a hilltop in Stow. The architects that had built the home were a father and son who had immigrated from Scandinavia. This home was the transmutation into reality of their dreams. It had an exercise room on the first floor, a spacious study on the middle floor, and a top floor with a built-in jacuzzi. In the center, an atrium extended all the way to the top floor. I crafted the details of my first business plan in this home.

It was reasonable to assume that there was a high demand for the high-tech corporations in the Route 128 area to expand overseas, so I directed my initial marketing efforts at the computer-related businesses here. My second target would be Fortune 500 companies on the East Coast.

My instincts turned out to be right on the mark. I received my first contract from the computer giant Digital Equipment Corporation (DEC) in Maynard, which had been founded by former MIT professor Kenneth Olsen. My job was to train a director, his family and staff scheduled to be stationed in Japan.

On this first job, I made an unfortunate cultural slip. My clients were incredibly cooperative, and to show my appreciation I offered them a discount on future training. Later, when I had the opportunity to take a look at the company's documents from back then, I happened upon the following comment regarding my work: "The inconsistency in this company's pricing indicates a lack of professionalism." This incident reveals significant differences between Japanese and American business practices.

After finding my first clients, building up a client base proved to be an arduous task. I thought endlessly about how to attract more business and what marketing strategies to employ. But no miracle solution presented itself.

One day I was in Boston's downtown area when I spotted the *Bay Side Area*, a free magazine providing information on local events. Then suddenly, it dawned on me. I could organize a series of seminars and advertise it in this magazine. The theme had to be of interest to Americans. The title I came up with was,

"Japan vs. the US Seminar Series

Sumo Wrestling and the Japanese Decision Making System: A Thorough Exploration of Their Differences from Decision Making in the US."

The advertisement caused quite a sensation, drawing a large audience. Encouraged by this initial success I continued to advertise weekly new seminars on topics **combining business management with Japanese arts or sports which Americans would also be familiar with.** These seminars gradually grew in popularity.

FEATURED IN TIME MAGAZINE

One day, out of the blue, I received a phone call from a TIME magazine reporter. "We are quite interested in your work and would like to interview you." Marveling at my good fortune, I could not resist letting out a whoop of joy.

The interview process was painstaking, as befitting a magazine of TIME's stature. First, they sent a freelance journalist to attend one of my seminars and submit a summary to the editor. Once the summary was approved, the writer visited me again, this time accompanied by a cameraman. Although only one photograph would eventually make its way into the magazine, the cameraman used roll after roll of color film to capture the quintessential shot.

Following the seminar, the writer interviewed me personally for ninety minutes. I thought they would be done by now, but I was wrong – next the team visited the company of each seminar participant to gather more information.

Finally, after laboriously verifying every word via telephone, the writer submitted a one-page article for review.

The completed article was entirely rewritten in its final stages by the chief editor, after which it went into print. I was astounded at how much effort and money was required for the publication of just one article. Even now, whenever I see a copy of TIME magazine, the memory of that interview springs immediately to mind.

After several delays, the article was finally published in TIME in the spring of 1985 with the title, "Zen in the Executive Suite". The response was outstanding. This being a time when the Internet had not yet come into existence, soon my phone was ringing off the hook, letters came pouring in, and people visited my office unexpectedly. Some of the requests generated by the publicity were rather bizarre. One odd query came from an individual raising 150 cattle in Chicago, who wanted to know how he could sell his products in Japan. Another client was seeking advice on how to establish a similar training company in India. Local newspapers and magazines were clamoring for more interviews. There were even invitations to create teaching materials.

In addition, we were now receiving inquiries from corporate clients interested in our services, which was what I had been eagerly hoping for. Requests for seminars came in one after another from well-known corporations such the IBM computer plant in Boca Raton, Florida, Xerox in Rochester, New York, and the Ford Motor headquarters in Dearborn, Michigan.

Although I had begun the training program as a business, it turned out that

I was regarded as an expert in this field, especially since I had been a researcher at Harvard. The only way for me to live up to those expectations was to immerse myself into serious study. I can honestly say that I had never studied as hard as I did at this time!

The demand continued over the next five years, testifying to the influence of TIME magazine. From a different perspective, however, there was clearly an urgent need for "cross-cultural management", a management style which would dig down to a cultural level to address the kind of problems that arise from doing business in foreign environments. Yet, at that time, no one offered services that could fill that need. As you would expect from a nationally acclaimed magazine, those at TIME had accurately identified this need in the business world.

THE EMERGENCE OF COMPETITION: MOVING ON TO THE NEXT STAGE

Unfortunately, this honeymoon period of no competition was only temporary. As a side effect of the extensive coverage we enjoyed in various media following the publication of the TIME article, competitors began to emerge.

In addition to seminars delivered at our clients' locations, we also offered monthly seminars open to the public. Well-known management schools and English language schools started sending their staff to attend the public seminars. Before long, these participants were using the skills they had learned to expand into the business market. As a result, cross-cultural management training spread like wildfire throughout the US.

Entering the market for cross-cultural management was considered easy. For example, there had been cases when an American who had spent only a year in Spain would, upon returning to the US, position himself as an authority on Spanish culture, and sometimes even as an expert in cross-cultural management at the global level. As such situations became increasingly common, I began to realize that some amount of curtailment was necessary.

I also knew that, in real business settings, merely understanding that different countries had different ways of doing things did not always lead to a final resolution. The "1980s model" of reaching an appreciation of cultural difference by comparing one's own country with the country of other actors involved in a business transaction had its limits. It was time to move to the next stage.

CHAPTER 2
THE ENCOUNTER WITH GLOBALIZATION, AND ITS TRANSFORMATIVE IMPACT

"HAVE YOU READ THE GLOBALIZATION ARTICLE?"

It was the spring of 1991, and I was conducting a seminar on cross-cultural management at the DuPont headquarters in Delaware. As I was taking a quick break in the company lounge, a middle-aged woman in charge of the training came bustling in. In her hand was a copy of the latest *Harvard Business Review*. "Have you read this article?" she asked. It was an issue devoted to global managers. One article in particular, titled "The Logic of Global Business", caught my eye. Nowadays, the term "global business" is commonplace, but at the time it still carried a ring of novelty and freshness.

The article was an interview with Percy Barnevik, the CEO of ABB Group, a company headquartered in Switzerland. Barnevik talked about how he had forged ABB through the merger of the Swedish company Asea with the Swiss Brown Boveri, and later expanded to build a potent global enterprise. Even today, ABB Group remains one of the world's leaders in electrical power and automation technologies.

Although at the time tension was melting, the Soviet Union was still in place and the Cold War era had yet to come to an end. The collapse of the Soviet Union six months later marked what many call the dawn of the global age. In reality however, global corporations had already begun emerging in Europe prior to this landmark event. The article in the *Harvard Business Review* conveyed a palpable sense that a new era was coming into existence.

This realization profoundly impacted me.

America was actually lagging behind Europe. While it was clear that the United States would eventually prevail in the Cold War, many corporate leaders contented themselves with savoring the sweet nectar of victory, and did little to prepare for the new beginnings headed their way. As a consultant for large American corporations, such as DuPont, IBM, and United Technologies (UTC), I was well in tune with the thinking of US corporate leaders. In Europe however a new age was dawning, with Percy Barnevik treading gallantly at the forefront.

I had a vision of the world as an enormous chessboard about to be rearranged. This was exactly what I had been wishing for all these years: an opportunity to do work that would be part of such sweeping processes of rearrangement. I can honestly say that it was Percy Barnevik's example that inspired me to venture into the field of global education while in the US, and later fueled my audacious hopes of bringing true globalization to Japan to make it a more competitive world player. I am indebted beyond words to the CEO of ABB Group, for his tremendously open mind, and for the outstanding global corporation model which he perfected and made available worldwide.

A DRASTICALLY CHANGING WORLD

The world was indeed on the verge of major change. In 1995, the World Trade Organization (WTO) was formed as the successor to the General Agreement on Tariffs and Trade (GATT). Further progress was made with the adoption of the Agreement on Technical Barriers to Trade, commonly referred to as the TBT Agreement, an international set of standards that prohibits discriminatory practices in trade. These were the first clear steps taken to establish a set of common rules for fair competition among companies around the world.

I will never forget the astonishment I felt when, one year later, I first learned about the World Wide Web (WWW) and the global reach of its hypertext system. Both the efforts to standardize international business rules and the rise of instant communication networks via the Internet were clear indications of a shift. The world was moving, perceptibly and irreversibly, towards globalization.

Following my encounter with globalization, I was impatient to take action. The problem, however, was finding out where to begin. First, I attempted to sell my services to various corporations in order to establish a stable flow of profit. In particular, I poured my efforts into convincing the global chemical giant DuPont and Hartford, Connecticut-based UTC to list my program in their seminar catalogues. This came at a time when DuPont had run into a number of problems with foreign governments, making the need for cross-cultural management more urgent than ever. UTC, a large corporation with numerous blue chip subsidiaries under its umbrella, was in turn going through a period of transition. Whereas before they had relied exclusively on large defense contracts from the federal government, they now needed to shift to commercially-based business targeting private corporations. Changing the way of thinking of these American executives once dependent on the defense industry was no easy task, but nonetheless a golden opportunity.

In the end, both corporations agreed to adopt the program. For the next fifteen years, they would serve as testing grounds for my experiments in global education. My experience *navigating* the depths of the corporate world at this particular temporal juncture shaped my understanding of what educating global talent was really all about. Rather than just skimming the surface, I had to navigate in real time through the entrails of a multi-dimensional world configured by the axes of time and space. What follows is an account of the world that this journey revealed, and of the insights I gained in the process.

THE EMERGING WORLD MARKET AND THE CREATION OF A NEW BUSINESS MODEL

In one sense, the training program in country-focused cross-cultural business at DuPont stood in sharp contrast to that of UTC. On numerous occasions, I offered seminars at UTC's Leadership Center, a facility providing training for the executives of the company's subsidiaries. I soon noticed that each one of these executives was fiercely independent; they each wanted to lord over their own castle. The companies they ran were world leaders in their respective fields – be it the manufacturing of jet engines, helicopters, air conditioners, or elevators. But they showed no intention of integrating into a global corporation.

On the other hand, DuPont was more proactive. What I proposed to DuPont at that point was what I call a "glass cleaning strategy". By having staff from two different countries learning about the other country's way of doing business, both sides of the "glass" are wiped clean. As a result, both teams move forward in mutual understanding, and their business competencies are enhanced.

To elaborate these strategies, I was invited to visit subsidiary companies in several European countries, Korea, Japan, Mexico, and other locations, where I had the opportunity to enrich my knowledge of how the corporation operated worldwide. With the appointment of Chad Holliday Jr. as CEO, DuPont embarked on wave after wave of mergers and acquisitions in pursuit of further expansion, reinforcing my perception that the world had become analogous to a chessboard. I designed programs for joint ventures with companies in countries around the world, including Turkey, Mexico, Brazil, and Taiwan. I also contracted local instructors to develop and deliver the curriculum.

During this period, every day was a battle for survival in the business world. In the early 1980s, when I moved to the US, I encountered a widespread stereotype of the Japanese as being particularly skillful at imitating and copying the West. To counter that negative reputation, the motto I lived by was "100% original content." My goal was to create completely original seminars not offered anywhere else. On an almost daily basis, I stayed up studying or discussing the training details with the instructors until the early hours of the morning. The program was so thorough that one of the instructors, an African-American man with an MBA from Harvard Business School and a PhD in law, told me he learned more during our collaboration than he had at Harvard!

The project that captivated me most at the time was developing a model that treated the world as one marketplace. In those days, customer understanding and the ability to meet a diversity of market needs were emerging as important themes. In the US, the term diversity was closely related to the problem of equal employment, which stemmed from the human rights movement of the 1960s. I, however, interpreted it more broadly as a problem of customer diversity in the world market. First, I grouped country-based comparisons together by region, and came up with seven major regions that I used as a basis for further comparison. Then, I discussed the resulting diagram with our team of international instructors. This enabled me to improve the accuracy of the representation and to obtain a panoramic understanding of the world, producing a world market model that could be used both in global marketing and local staff management. This was such enjoyable work that I often lost track of time, immersing myself fully in the project.

AN EYE-OPENING EXPERIENCE OF DIVERSITY AT IBM

I believe it was in 1997 when I was selected to manage an "experimental training seminar for diverse leaders" at IBM's Multicultural Leadership Center in North Carolina. My rival for this project was a company managed by a Caucasian couple and comprised of mostly Caucasian staff. In contrast, my company was a literal plethora of racial diversity, featuring instructors from almost thirty different countries. IBM, a company with a venerable history, declared us the winners.

When I visited IBM to discuss the project, I understood why they had chosen us. A young staff member who was in charge of personnel affairs greeted me with a handshake, saying, "Nice to meet you. I'm a lesbian." IBM had undergone a radical metamorphosis, redefining itself as a corporation that was the epitome of diversity.

The goal of the seminar was to select 150 staff members representing various dimensions of diversity, such as gender, sexual preference, and ethnic background, who would all go through the same leadership training. The results would be evaluated at the end of the program. The implementation of the project also doubled as training for IBM's younger staff, and therefore required an extraordinary amount of time and effort. However, the payoff proved worthwhile since the training was a huge success. The course was taught by a team of instructors with truly diverse backgrounds, including a French national born in Africa, as well as Chinese, Egyptian, Peruvian, African-American, and Japanese trainers. We taught IBM's young employees, many of whom were locals from the North Carolina region, about the key elements necessary for success in both domestic and global leadership arenas.

Our work earned us our client's recognition. About two months later I received a call from the IBM headquarters in Armonk, New York. "We are planning to establish a global committee for personnel affairs which will bring together HR managers from Asia, Europe, South America, and North America. Your company's name came up in our planning discussions." When I asked what other training providers IBM was considering, they mentioned the Dutch consulting business Trompenaars Hampden-Turner (THT). (THT is now part of the KPMG international People & Change Practice). I felt immensely honored to be standing next to such a prestigious organization, a company which had positioned itself at the vanguard of the industry with the publication as early as 1993 of the best-seller *Riding the Waves of Culture* by Fons Trompenaars and Charles Hampden-Turner.

Although IBM ended up choosing THT, through this experience I realized the level of competitiveness that my company had reached. This gave me a renewed sense of self-confidence.

TRAVELLING AROUND THE WORLD WITH THE NCR PROJECT

In the year 2000, I was commissioned by NCR's US headquarters to work on a project involving the worldwide introduction of IT systems. It was a project that literally had me traveling all over the world. NCR had been acquired at one point by AT&T, but eventually regained its status as a freestanding company, a move indicating their determination to keep the company independent. Every single issue raised in the NCR project continues to hold relevance for the globalization agenda today. Below are some of the questions that the project sought to address:

- The IT system designed at our headquarters is the product of an American style of thinking. How can it be converted into a global product?
- To what extent can subsidiaries in each country disclose the IT information of local clients, banks, etc.? How could one bring about improvements in countries with low levels of corporate openness and accountability?
- What features of communication and approval processes need to be taken into account when convincing decision-makers in each country to adopt an IT system?
- In the EU and Latin America, it is important to consider differences between what world-system theory calls core and peripheral countries. How can we ensure that information sharing and work distribution are carried out fairly and equitably?
- Up to now, an enormous amount of time, effort, and money has been

used to resolve problems caused by simple miscommunication and cultural misunderstandings. Can companies increase work speed, lower costs, and raise competitiveness if all staff adopt a global perspective, and strengthen communication and virtual teamwork?

As executive staff heard the reviews of this seminar they also joined in, and finally we decided to hold a seminar tailored exclusively for executive staff. The work I did for NCR helped greatly in expanding my knowledge and experience of globalization in the business world, and of the various problems associated with it.

Besides NCR, over 95% of my clients were top-level multinational corporations. If I were to list all the places my work took me in the decade of the 1990s, it would seem like I was soaring around the world. The regions I traveled to were primarily North America, Asia, Oceania, and Europe. Unfortunately, I was never requested to conduct training in South America, the Middle East, or Africa. But given that clients from these regions often came to North America and Asia to learn, in total I had the opportunity to work with people from well over thirty countries.

JAPANESE AND AMERICAN NOTIONS OF TEAMWORK ARE PROFOUNDLY DIFFERENT

During this time, I had numerous interesting experiences, a few of which I would like to share in concluding this chapter.

I received my first request to teach an on-site seminar in the US from the Xerox Training Institute in Rochester, New York. Bausch & Lomb and Kodak, who were located nearby, were also my clients, and so my trips between Boston and Rochester became so frequent that I had to use a commuter pass. As I was led into the Xerox training room, I noticed posters on the walls everywhere reading "Teamwork is important". It was just like being in Japan! I felt optimistic that our talks would go smoothly, but I was wrong. I later came to realize that the word "teamwork" had a fundamentally different meaning for the corporation's American team as opposed to their Japanese team. So I created a model to explain these differences in an effective manner and spent time ensuring they were properly understood.

As this example illustrates, it is quite common for the same term to be used with different meanings in different cultural regions. There are also frequent cases of words with almost the same dictionary definition yet which may be perceived as complete opposites in certain cultural regions. Assuming that the terms used in a discussion convey unambiguous meaning for all parties can lead to serious misunderstandings.

After I finished the seminar at Xerox and returned to the lounge room, the training director asked me if there had been many questions. The seminar had indeed spurred many questions, so I responded in the affirmative, feeling embarrassed that the participants had a hard time understanding the material because of my inadequate teaching skills. However, I learned later that in America, the ability to provoke questions from the participants was evidence of a seminar's success. I understood that my way of seeing things was still trapped in Japanese patterns of value judgment.

AN IBM EXECUTIVE APOLOGIZES

At the end of the summer of 1985, I was invited to the IBM computer manufacturing plant in Boca Raton, Florida. The seminar was intended for an audience of male executives who considered themselves elite - a stark contrast to the diverse environment of IBM today. I remember thinking, "So these are the people referred to as WASP (White, Anglo-Saxon, Protestant)!"

The Japanese side was having difficulties selling IBM's high-performance computers, so now the US executives had to jump on board to teach them how to sell. They had requested the seminar for this reason. The belief that all markets are the same, despite the different cultures enframing them, and that selling methods in foreign markets are ineffective is a common misperception even today. The situation demanded a nuanced understanding of cross-cultural business.

I started by explaining the Japanese principle of putting the customer first, the meaning of after-sales service, the distribution system, usability of computers designed to US specifications, and part replacement, drawing detailed comparisons between the American and the Japanese markets. I also touched upon cultural differences. For instance, I discussed the centrality of interpersonal relationships to doing business in Japan, and stressed the cultural importance of apologizing not only for obvious mistakes, but also for any inconvenience caused to customers.

At that moment, one of the participants suddenly got up and left the room without a word, and did not return for some time. As I continued teaching the seminar, I thought he must have been really displeased with the content. But even so, how rude of him to leave like that…

About forty minutes later, the participant returned. "I thought I'd better send an apology telex to my Japanese customers sooner rather than later," he said.

Two or three of his colleagues chuckled as someone remarked, "Now this is something one doesn't hear every day. The Captain apologized!" Another chimed in, "That might be the first apology he has ever made!"

FORD CORPORATION'S STRONG SENSE OF PRIDE

While some found my arguments persuasive, there were also others who were less willing to suspend what they deemed "common sense". Once, I was speaking at an executive seminar at Ford headquarters in Dearborn, Michigan. During the session, one person asked, "We want to sell more cars in Asia – especially in Japan. How should we go about doing that?" The suggestions I offered included putting the steering wheel on the right side of the car instead of the left, making smaller cars that would suit Japan's narrow roads, and developing competitive intelligence by studying Toyota's automobile production system, in particular its close collaboration with subcontractors. However, I noticed that while I was speaking those present starting casting their eyes downward, and finally one director, unable to contain his anger, spoke out. "It's easy to say that we should change the position of the steering wheel. But do you have any idea how much that would cost us?" At the time, Ford Motors was still at the height of its glory, and this was reflected in its directors' pride.

Seven years later, I received word that Ford Motors had hired a university professor and automobile industry expert from California to implement all of the changes I had recommended. I realized that whenever my reasoning was correct, at some point it would be proven so, and that, if my ideas occasionally appeared out of place, it was because they were several years ahead of their time. This instilled in me a self-confidence bordering on audacity.

CHAPTER 3
THE WORLD REVEALS ITSELF IN THE CULTURE FACTOR

Tools for Understanding Global Business

KEY INFORMATION FOR GLOBAL SUCCESS?

Having decided to develop a global market model, my first task was to determine what information was essential to business success. This quest drew my attention to the role of ethnic identity and cultural DNA.

With the collapse of the Cold War ideological structure of liberalism versus communism, ethnic identity emerged to the foreground as an important value. A general understanding of the distinctive identities that individuals claim for themselves can, therefore, facilitate both client development and the management of local staff. Indeed, this understanding is indispensable as a business support tool in today's global age.

With this in mind, I began browsing through existing literature on the subject, but, much to my dismay, found that there was nothing written on the particular issues that concerned me. Seeing no other alternative, I decided to devise my own model, which ultimately led to the creation of the Cultural World Map™ and Global Navigator™. I shall return to these tools in more detail later, but first I would like to outline briefly the process that I followed in developing them. Without a doubt, they were the direct products of my experience navigating amidst the world's major ethnic identities and cultural DNAs.

Although religion is commonly used as a proxy for categorizing the world into cultures in order to make sense of it, I deliberately avoided this approach. In so doing, I was following the advice of an acquaintance who was an education professional in the US, and who had warned me to avoid explicit references to religion when designing teaching materials for use in schools around the world.

What I used instead was a "time axis". I created a matrix by combining the spatial axis of the world with a five-thousand-year time axis. This time span was chosen because the Chinese people consider their country's history to date back five thousand years. The timeline of Judaism, which is said to extend for four thousand years, would not have worked for considering China. Wanting to make these tools easily applicable in business, I compiled the information by country rather than by major ethnic groups. When doing business with a specific country, one needs to be aware of the traditions local people value, but there are few who can give a concise and accurate account of their own culture. Learning systematically about the other party's culture on one's own would, however, require an enormous investment of time. My solution to this dilemma was to illustrate each country's traditions along a time axis that was summarized in a one-page sheet.

Rather than following a chronological format, the document represented the various periods as cultural layers, showing how they emerged and vanished from ancient times to the present. I included dotted lines to delineate wars, colonization, and other major traumatic events, advising caution in approaching such topics. However, these materials served merely to provide historical data. Finding ways to convey the values specific to particular cultural areas was a more complex challenge.

CHAPTER 3: THE WORLD REVEALS ITSELF IN THE CULTURE FACTOR

The problem is that by making definitive statements about certain groups of people, you immediately create stereotypes. I needed to avoid such essentializing portrayals at all costs. After pondering the issue for several months, I finally came to the conclusion that a productive way to start was to consider the cultural factors that motivate or offend each group. Posing these questions could effectively bring to the foreground important aspects of the culture we were examining. I named these key aspects cultural motivators and cultural demotivators (See page 121 for further details).

WORKING TOGETHER WITH INSTRUCTORS FROM AROUND THE WORLD

I could now see the direction in which I was heading. However, in between travelling around the world and running my business, it would take me five and a half more years to bring these tools to completion. If, in the end, I managed to mold them into a finished product, it was thanks to the talented instructors who helped me in this process.

In the late 1990s, one of the main objectives on my company's agenda was to recruit highly qualified instructors from a diverse range of countries, and forge a team that would be able to offer corporate seminars of outstanding value. At first, I relied on my connections from Harvard and other prominent local universities. In those days, the tumultuous changes that would eventually lead to the breakdown of the Cold War order had brought an avalanche of foreign intellectuals into the US, many of whom were equipped with advanced academic degrees. It was, it turned out, surprisingly easy to hire high-caliber personnel. These immigrants sought readily available income, and teaching seminars at large corporations had the added appeal of allowing a certain flexibility in terms of time commitment. Of course, holding an advanced degree did not instantly make these individuals effective instructors. We, therefore, entered a tacit cooperation agreement: I would provide them with the knowhow required to teach the seminars in exchange for them helping me create a global cultural navigation tool broken down by country.

THE DIFFICULT BIRTH OF THE CULTURAL WORLD MAP

This is how the process unfolded. In a first stage, we conducted interviews with local people. For countries that our American clients were less likely to be familiar with, we selected native instructors who were holders of PhD degrees to act as interviewers. Interviews in the better-known countries were carried out by groups of experts. Then, interviewers analyzed the case studies they had collected, adding commentary based on their own knowledge and experience to produce the first drafts. In the next stage, a committee consisting of instructors and clients from various countries discussed these drafts at length.

The instructor team brought to the table a rich mix of idiosyncratic backgrounds. It included a Russian-Ukrainian couple, both PhD holders, who had come to the US following the collapse of the Soviet Union; a business professional who had fled political unrest in the Balkan Peninsula, living in three countries before finally settling down in the US; a former senior government official from Beijing, who had fallen out with his superior and, fearing for his own safety, escaped to the US; a Taiwanese engineer who had married an American citizen while working in the US; a researcher from India; a Mexican who had studied at an American graduate school and, after having returned to his native land for a while, was now back in the US; a professor from Argentina who had transferred to an American university together with his wife because of a deteriorating economy at home...

Because the idea of a Global Navigator was new, even these intellectuals had a hard time grasping its significance as I envisioned it. Most of the time, the drafts were not exactly what I needed. Ultimately, I had to assume responsibility for overseeing the whole process, making the necessary revisions and final adjustments to the material they submitted. But the enormous amount of effort that went into this process made it a powerful learning experience. I also realized that the more I thought about cultural identities in other countries, the more I found myself drawing comparisons with the Japanese identity. As a result, creating these tools helped me attained an even deeper understanding of the Japanese and their culture.

DO ASIA AND SOUTH AMERICA SHARE A SIMILAR SENSE OF VALUES?

In the course of this work of identifying each country's cultural DNA and articulating it around the dual axes of space and time, I noticed that certain regions and countries could be grouped together by shared values. Even more remarkably, the process of categorization often resulted in rather unconventional groupings.

A particular incident made me acutely aware of the implications of this finding. Almost concurrently, I received requests from separate corporations to design two seminars – one on doing business in Asia, the other on doing business in Latin America. It was a time when world politics and economies were already undergoing major changes as globalization was gathering pace. Among the most conspicuous changes were the emergence of the Association of Southeast Asian Nations (ASEAN) and of Asian markets including China, as well as the rise of the Latin American market in the aftermath of the confusion caused by the enactment in January 1994 of the North American Free Trade Agreement (NAFTA). These developments led to increased demand for business in both of these regions.

While working in tandem on these projects with Latin American and Asian instructors, we realized that the essentials of the curriculum could be transferred in almost identical format from one seminar to another. A member of the Latin American team laughed saying, "Just use the same format. You don't need to tell the client – create one format and receive the design fee from both companies." But I could not laugh. Rather than finding humor in the situation, I was bemused to find that two regions that are so vastly distinct would possess remarkably similar values.

The more I reflected on this new discovery, the more evident it was that the Asian and Latin American instructors in many cases *did* share similar values. For example, their aversion and resistance towards contracts – many of these instructors appeared displeased when asked to sign an employment contract in the hiring process. Nowadays more people understand the need for contracts, but at that time many Latin Americans and Asians new to the US believed that contracts should be entered into after developing a relationship with their contract partner. To persuade them, I grounded my arguments in American values, as if I myself had been an American citizen: "I completely understand your concerns, but this is America and procedures are the exact opposite. You first enter into a contract, then work on building a relationship of trust. To begin with, you cannot work at companies in America if you don't first sign an employment contract and a nondisclosure agreement." After such an explanation, some would find more excuses to delay signing.

Others would say, "Ms. Atsumi, I am signing this contract because I trust you. If any problems arise, I trust that you will see that they are resolved." Then, they would put their signature on the contract with an attitude of leaving all matters to my discretion. While it was impossible to start business with the former, the latter's tendency to defer responsibility could also become a terrible burden when doing business in the US. Both of these types were troublesome to deal with.

OUR DIFFERENCES ARE THE PRODUCT OF WHAT WE CONSIDER OUR CORE VALUES!

In a sense, the American value system, with its emphasis on rules and know-how, and value systems based on the teaching of God, such as those of the Islamic cultural sphere, were easy to understand. However, even I was uncertain about how to approach Asia, Latin America, and former communist countries. I really needed to take advantage of this new insight regarding possible similarities between Latin America and Asia to compare the value indices of the seven major regions of Asia, Oceania, Europe, the Middle East, Africa, North America, and Latin America, and see if the data backed my hypothesis.

With this thought I gathered together my team of instructors residing in the Boston vicinity. The team consisted of two instructors who were Catholic Latin Americans, two, including me, from the region of Asia influenced by Confucianism, two Americans, one from India, and one Muslim, who had joined as a virtual team member. We compared the regions across a number of indicators and came to the conclusion that, when core values for Asia and Latin America were consolidated on a larger scale, they matched almost perfectly.

The indicators that we used in this exercise included business styles (is priority given to regulations and professional expertise or to interpersonal relations?), vertical vs. horizontal organizational relations, spatial approaches (learning models that progress from the center to the overall picture, or vice versa?), temporal approaches (linear or circular conceptions of time?), communication styles (nonverbal, indirect "high-context" communication or more explicit and assertive "low context" communication?), and mentality (black-or-white or a gradation of shades of grey?).

The realization that Asia and Latin America shared similar values caused gasps throughout the room, as we exchanged glances with each other. It was already late and all that could be seen outside was the pitch black of night. Up to that point we had visualized the world in terms of maps showing the distribution of religions, and so we had not expected to find such parallels between the values and thought patterns that occur in Catholic and Confucian cultural regions.

"Do you think it's acceptable to classify Catholic and Confucian regions together as stratified societies centered on interpersonal relations?"

"We're going to get an earful from believers and scholars of religion."

"Listen, I'm catholic, but I think that there is no reason why we should refrain from using this finding. After all, what we are trying to do here is to develop effective business tools that will facilitate an understanding of the values and thought patterns of people around the world."

"As long as we continue to use conventional categories to divide the world up into Christianity versus Confucianism, the East will remain East and the West, West. We'll never be rid of stereotypes of an insurmountable difference between the two. By showing that the same categories can be used to describe both Confucian and Catholic regions, we are actually proposing a new perspective, a new way of thinking about the world that is better suited to these times of globalization."

"Throughout history, we have killed each other in the name of differences in religion and ethnicity. But our differences are, ultimately, the product of what we consider to be our core values. If we understood that from the very beginning, and could discern the value systems at work in different places, there would be no need for us to be killing each other. The contribution that we could make to spreading this message is more than reason enough to create this map!" An excited buzz enveloped the room as everyone began voicing their ideas. It was the beginning of a conversation that would lead to the creation of the Cultural World Map - a world map for today's global age.

TRACING HISTORY THROUGH THE EYES OF CHILDREN TO CREATE A COMMON WORLDWIDE EDUCATIONAL PROGRAM

When the World Trade Center attack occurred on September 11, 2001, I was in New York City with my family. It took a while for me to register that those scenes of spectacular destruction, which seemed straight out of a Hollywood movie, were for real. My daughter had been headed for LaGuardia Airport for a business trip to Mexico, only to find the airport closed. She returned home not even knowing what was going on. My son-in-law was unable to come home from the Goldman Sachs headquarters, not far away from Ground Zero. However, the real horror began the following day. Terrorists might attack George Washington Bridge… The Holland Tunnel was in danger… Nuclear power plants were being targeted…. With daily television reports highlighting levels of risk for each area on a color-coded scale, focusing on work became nearly impossible. We spent those days loading drinking water and emergency food rations into cars, as we waited for announcements from the community informing us that we needed to evacuate.

The world had entered an age of war on terror. But what could be done to reduce terror? Through multiple conversations with friends and family members working in international business, I came to realize that, although reaching a solution would require time, what was needed was a common education for children worldwide. Of course, it is important to have education that nurtures a sense of cultural and national identity. On the other hand, children should be taught from a young age that they live in a diverse world characterized by a plurality of values, ways of thinking, and physical appearances. Teaching materials such as the Cultural Word Map, which vividly illustrated the world's diversity, would play an essential role in this education process.

The World Trade Center attack served as a wake-up call for the US. Not only school administrators and educators, but also parents became obsessed with the idea that a US-centric education was no longer sufficient and changes had to be made. However, the debate about how this could be accomplished had so far been limited to proposals for integrating cultural studies into foreign language education. They used a narrow notion of diversity to signify differences among the foods people ate in countries such as Mexico or France, the clothes they wore and the languages they spoke. I, however, saw things differently. Rather than a piecemeal approach to the understanding of diversity, what was needed was a more radical and holistic educational program.

Two and a half years later, I founded a company which specialized in global education for children. Its staff members were an international team of instructors representing the US, Japan, England, and Singapore.

Irrespective of their parents' political ideology, religion or ethnicity, children around the world were capable, if they so desired, of creating a common platform for mutual understanding. My wish was to create a program that got such a message across. What emerged out of these explorations was a program called "Ten Steps to Reach the Global Village™." The program drew an enthusiastic response not only in the US but in Japan as well, where it was developed into a textbook for high school students.

Working on this program was an eye-opening experience. Global corporate training focuses on what is happening in the world at the moment. However, the experience that the "Ten Steps to Reach the Global Village™" program was designed to enable was precisely one of *navigating* the world across time and space.

As I explained in chapter two, one of the lessons I learned from my forays into the business world was that, in order to become a truly global professional, extensive traveling was insufficient. One had to navigate the world to foster the modes of thinking needed to face head on the rapid processes of globalization. The "Ten Steps to Reach the Global Village™" program was just that - a simulated experience of navigating the world.

THREE ATTRIBUTES OF INFLUENTIAL GLOBAL LEADERS

Having been active for many years in global education has allowed me to see that individuals who can be referred to as "global leaders" share certain distinguishing attributes – features that transcend ethnicity, age, and gender. These attributes can be summarized as follows:

1) They boldly engage with the world in its entirety.
2) They navigate the world.
3) They are able to discern that which has so far escaped attention, and to form a clear idea of the changes that the world needs.

First, being able to engage with the world in its entirety is a crucial departure point. Traditional learning processes have tended to start with the study of one's self and one's own country and later expand to include the broader world. However, this order is the exact opposite of how we actually acquire knowledge, an issue that we will consider later in this book.

The next key trait is the skill of navigating the world. While the importance of personal experience cannot be understated, for those looking for concrete hints on how to perfect this art I recommend reading the biographies of accomplished global leaders, to see how they went about their journeys.

The final point is a corollary of the first two: it is as a result of their engagement with the world in its fullness, and of their experience navigating it, that

CHAPTER 3: THE WORLD REVEALS ITSELF IN THE CULTURE FACTOR

global leaders become able to discern that which has so far escaped attention, and to form a clear idea of the changes that are needed.

However, what sort of person does the term "global leader" describe? Some of the names that come readily to mind are IBM chairman and CEO Louis Gerstner, Samsung Group chairman Lee Kun-hee, Renault/Nissan chairman and CEO Carlos Ghosn, Microsoft founder Bill Gates, or Grameen Bank founder Muhammad Yunus. These individuals all possess the three attributes mentioned above, starting with the ability to think in terms of the big picture. One does not have to be a rare genius to take up such a stance, since it will empower any ordinary citizen to become a driving force of change. And, furthermore, to create innovation in large-scale organizations, relying on a steadfast wisdom that reaches beyond religion or violence. This shift in perspective is significant because it marks a key difference between the prerequisites for being a business professional up until the twentieth century and those for being one in today's global world.

Such individuals, who shoulder the weight of current global conditions, as they strive to effect changes through their work, typically remain grounded and humble. To this day, I have never encountered a global leader who erred on the side of arrogance.

Do not feel discouraged by this imposing assembly of eminent figures, believing you could never possibly emulate them. Think of Canadian Severn Suzuki, who addressed the delegates at the Rio United Nations Earth Summit, urging adults from every nation on the planet to stop breaking the Earth, if they did not know how to fix it. Recall the story of Craig Kielburger, the young man who was so outraged by a newspaper article about the murder of a child activist in Pakistan, that he flew to South Asia, and has ever since worked to end child labor and provide education for impoverished children globally. These individuals are, without a doubt, global leaders, and what is particularly striking is that they began their inspiring careers in activism and advocacy when they were just twelve years old! Their trajectories provide ample evidence that there are no age or gender limitations to being a global leader.

CHAPTER 4
UNDERSTANDING THE TRUE MEANING OF GLOBALIZATION
A Copernican Revolution in Perspectives and Ideas

WHAT IS GLOBALIZATION?

I hope those reading this account of half of my life have found it helpful in grasping certain trends in globalization over the last few decades. The present chapter draws out the implications of our discussion so far, reconsidering the definition of globalization and the reasons why the Japanese have had a hard time understanding this idea. Although a frequently used term, globalization is a rather fuzzy and ill-defined concept in Japan. This lack of clarity has likely prevented Japan from effectively responding to globalization.

What are we talking about, exactly, when we speak of globalization? The term "globalization" is derived from the English word "globe," meaning "celestial sphere," in this case, the Earth. In other words, globalization is an awareness of the Earth as a unit – a perspective or way of thinking that concerns itself with processes unfolding on a planetary scale.

A common mistake the Japanese make is using the terms "globalization" and "internationalization" interchangeably, with little regard for a nuanced understanding of the two. In his book *Global Standards: An Easy Guide* (Chukei Publishing, 1998) author Toshitake Chino draws a clear distinction between the international and the global, arguing that

- The international refers to (primarily bilateral) relationships between

states. It is grounded in the national logic of the nation-state.
- The global designates multilateral relationships. It is grounded in the global logic of the Earth as a whole.

Chino considers globalization as a stage in the evolution of internationalization, but draws attention to the entirely different nuances and connotations that this new stage possesses. However, since the term "evolution" may give the false impression that the internationalization stage has already become obsolete, I prefer to use the following definitions in distinguishing between these terms.

- International = Approaches, perspectives and movements that see the world in terms of relationships between countries, taking the "country" as their unit of analysis.
- Global = Approaches, perspectives and movements that see the world as a whole, taking the Earth as their unit of analysis.
    1)

For many people, speaking of "the Earth as unit" conjures up images of the terrestrial globe. This association effectively serves as the visual representation of a unit in its entirety, but it has the disadvantage of detracting from the real power of this phrase.

The power of globalization radiates from within; it expands as one leaves one's own country and becomes involved with other countries. It coexists with an awareness that, when viewed from space, the Earth is nothing more than a minuscule speck, a lonely point of light among the countless points of light that fill the vast enveloping cosmic dark. This dual vision frames my personal understanding of globalization. Simply put, it is important to grasp globalization as occurring along the two axes of time and space.

The key here is to understand that "international" and "global" are two very different concepts.

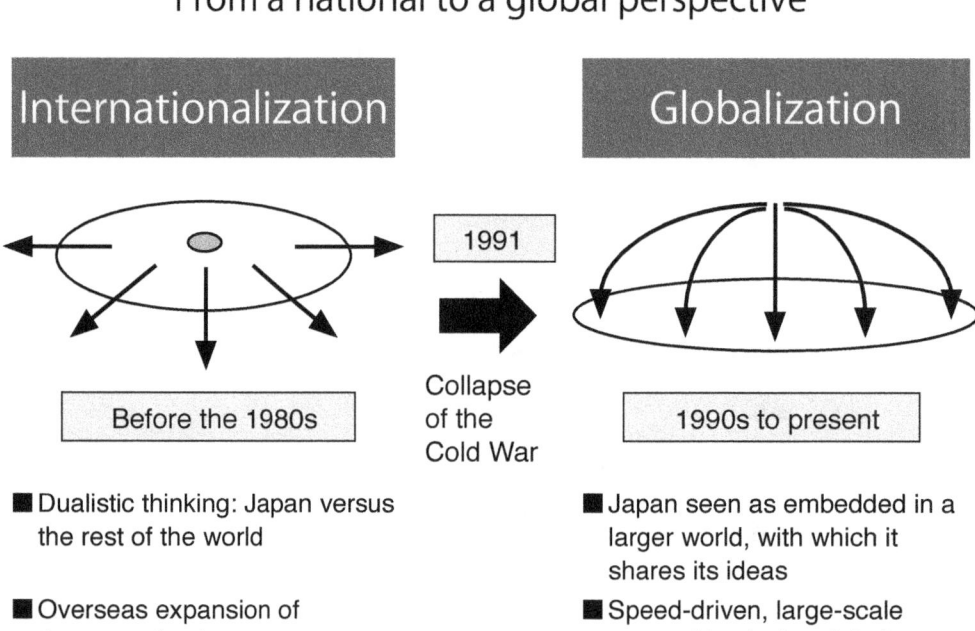

What is Globalization?
From a national to a global perspective

JAPAN'S FAILURE TO EMBRACE A GLOBAL MODEL

Why is this distinction important? One hint can be found in Japan's failure to shift from an international to a global model, which caused the country to stumble following its remarkable success in the 1980s (see the figure above). In the decade of the 1980s, Japan experienced an internationalization boom. The defining feature of internationalization during this period was the drive to expand domestic business overseas, which was rooted in a Japan-versus-the-outside-world dichotomy. This led to a flood of Japanese products pouring into overseas markets, which generated unprecedented economic prosperity in Japan.

It is true, though, that there were numerous cases of friction and antagonism, including trade wars and conflicts among headquarters and subsidiaries located in different countries. The following factors lay at the root of these problems.

- A country-focused perspective, which prevented Japan from engaging with the world in its entirety (seeing the big picture) and from acting strategically;
- The absence of unified rules and global standards;
- Japanese actors' insufficient awareness of their own limitations and of the cultural glasses through which they viewed their partners (relying exclusively on their own evaluation criteria);
- A tendency to favor countries and ethnic groups where headquarters were located, which made it difficult to motivate and secure long-term commitment from local foreign staff.

In the meantime, the world was transitioning to a global model in the aftermath of the collapse of the Soviet Union. In reality, it was the Space Race that began in the 1960s between the US and the Soviet Union which made it possible for humans everywhere to see the Earth from space. The continuous efforts of the United Nations to tackle environmental issues on a global scale have also contributed significantly to the formation of a global awareness. Such developments rapidly surfaced following the dissolution of the Soviet Union.
Another phenomenon occurred for the first time in human history during

this period: the emergence of a world market governed by the market principle. At the same time, progress was made setting clearer business rules, codes of practice and global standards. Examples include the expansion of the areas covered by the prescriptions of the International Organization for Standardization (ISO) and the establishment of the World Trade Organization (WTO) to replace the General Agreement on Tariffs and Trade (GATT). These initiatives have been intended to create rules for free and fair participation and competition in the world market.

This global model is characterized by the presence of a large, integrated market and the use of a bird's eye view perspective on its workings. Since domestic markets are no more than pieces in this global market puzzle, it is important to take an understanding of the whole world as our starting point.

For Japan, this would mean first arriving at a grasp of the current state of the world market, and then using this knowledge to reflect back upon itself and develop original products and models that can make a valuable contribution to the world.

This global model has the potential to resolve the problems that beset internationalization in the 1980s for the following reasons.

- Understanding the world market as a whole (the big picture) creates the conditions for acting more strategically.
- The establishment of unified rules and standards enables fair competition.
- The bird's eye view of the world, coupled with the use of a multicultural lens, stimulates a critical awareness of the cultural glasses

characteristic of one's own country, resulting in a more objective view the world.
- With the integration of staff databases worldwide, it becomes possible to evaluate staff fairly according to ability. Also, conditions for promotion become transparent and shared throughout the company – all the way to top executives at headquarters.

Japan, however, has been unable to produce any viable alternatives to the conviction, common until the 1980s, that manufacturing high quality products and shipping them overseas was all it took to be successful. Recently, there are signs that attitudes in Japan are at long last changing, but meanwhile top corporations around the world, such as GE, IBM, Siemens, and Samsung have already adopted this global model, gaining a significant lead over Japanese corporations.

"EVERYTHING CHANGES"

How does business change when shifting to a global model? We could summarize the answer in one sentence: everything changes. Human resource needs change, and so do business styles. For example, take education. In the 1980s it was considered that an adequate understanding of the world could be obtained through the fragmentary study of the relevant countries and issues, with no concern for grasping the overall picture of the world. Furthermore, evaluations of other countries and ethnic groups were unavoidably mediated by one's own cultural glasses. This resulted in distorted perceptions of reality, leading the Japanese into the trap of either idealizing or disparaging their foreign partners.
Also, the goal of this learning was at most to "reach an understanding."

Translating this understanding into action to actually effect change was regarded as dangerous. Even today, this outdated model is used unquestioningly in Japanese school education, as well as in corporate training for new staff and staff going overseas.

In contrast, global education requires a combination of comprehensive abilities, originality, speed and action.

Comprehensive abilities, which will be discussed in more detail later, include the ability to optimize by using a matrix, strategic thinking, planning skills, the ability to deliver added value, the ability to generate next generation models, and global communication skills.

Originality is also important. In the global market arena, imitation is unacceptable. This is why an emphasis on the Japanese cultural DNA is crucial in efforts to educate future global professionals.

Also, while Japanese businesses excel in areas such as promptness in responding to clients, they often attract criticism from overseas partners for being painfully slow at making decisions and resolving problems. However, when a global-scale, bird's eye view is adopted, it becomes possible to identify more clearly what needs to be accomplished and by when, leading to improvements in the speed with which issues are addressed.

A final focus of global education is on action. In a global model the playing field is set, as are international standards and fair rules of conduct. This means that, as long as the appropriate strategy has been determined, action can be taken immediately, leading to success.

Considering the above, it is clear that approaches to sales, for instance, will have to undergo major changes. Up until the 1980s, one was expected to personally travel to the target country and work oneself to the bone on sale calls, rather than learn about these countries in a systematic manner. But in the current global era, different skills are valued. These include intellectual tactics for operating on the giant integrated market, skill in discerning aspects not readily visible to the naked eye, and powers of insight. What is at stake is no longer success in selling one or two products, but the ability to design mechanisms for selling large quantities in each transaction.

We may conclude, therefore, that the international model of the 1980s and the global model that emerged in the mid 1990s are not only dissimilar, but almost diametric opposites in every respect, from perspectives, to ideas, and to the actions they require.

New principles and rules following the great value shift of the mid 1990s

Age of capitalism →	Age of the knowledge economy
① Political ideology ② Vertical control based on authority and status (vertical criteria) ③ Hard power ④ Dualistic thinking ⑤ Country-specific rules ⑥ Exclusivism ⑦ Workers doing repetitive labor, functioning like pieces of machinery under the direction of a supervisor ⑧ The principle of capital and labor	① Cultural and ethnic identity ② Horizontal solidarity based on knowledge, know-how and experience (horizontal criteria) ③ Soft power ④ Optimization / Simultaneous introduction of opposite values ⑤ International standards, unification of rules ⑥ Inclusionism ⑦ Knowledge workers ⑧ Market and humanitarian principles

A SHIFT IN THOUGHT PATTERNS: USING A MATRIX

If someone from a future generation were to create a timeline, they might draw a vertical line around the year 1995, dividing it into an earlier capitalist era and a subsequent post-capitalist, knowledge industry era. This timeline would accurately reflect just how influential the mid-90s were in bringing about an upheaval in the world's economic and communication systems. The transformations that took place during this time included the advent of the

Internet, the revision of the Foreign Exchange and Foreign Trade Control Law in Japan, and the reforms dubbed the "Japanese Big Bang". It is now common knowledge that the changes wrought in our social systems during the decade of the 90s were on a par with those of the industrial revolution. The figure above shows how values around the world evolved during this brief span of time.

This fundamental reconfiguration of values has created a need for matrix thinking. To become a global professional, conceiving of the world along a single axis has become insufficient. Instead, one needs to be able to use two axes simultaneously.

So just how have the axes of values around the world changed? Let us examine these changes more closely.

 1) Cultural and ethnic identity

After the collapse of the Cold War system with its bipolar opposition between a free world and a totalitarian, communist world, the values that gained renewed salience were ethnic identity and cultural DNA. The two decades since the end of the Cold War have been marked by an upsurge of conflicts based on ethnic identities, as minority populations resisted being ruled by a different ethnic or religious group, and aspired to form their own countries. Incidentally, attempts to "take back" and revitalize Japan following the 2011 Great East Japan earthquake and tsunami appear belated from a global perspective.

Given this context, understanding cultural and ethnic identity is key to business success in a global era. The Cultural World Map, which will be discussed in greater detail later in this book, can play an important role in gaining such an understanding.

2) From vertical to horizontal indicators

After its defeat in World War II, Japan was such a homogeneous society that as many as 90% of the Japanese considered themselves middle class. On the flip side, when comparing themselves to others, the Japanese are unusually eager to use hierarchical (vertical) indicators. This kind of thinking, which invites an awareness of one's status as higher or lower than others, structures relationships between bosses and subordinates, parent and subsidiary companies, clients and subcontractors.

However, in a global era a far greater value is attached to horizontal comparisons. Vertical indicators, such as authority, status, and wealth no longer appear as relevant as they once did; it is the horizontal collaboration among diverse forms of knowledge, know-how, and experience that is now important. While vertical indicators create barriers, horizontal indicators create bonds.

For example, vertical relationships between developed and developing countries have crumbled with the rise of emerging economies, each with its own particular model, which are now interacting on a more level playing field with developed nations. While in Japan vertical divisions of labor still exist between parent and subsidiary companies, over the past decade overseas corporations have switched successfully to forms of horizontal specialization.

In cases of competitive bidding for infrastructure development projects financed by national governments, it has become difficult to award the entire contract to a single firm. Instead, it is becoming increasingly common for companies from different countries to form coalitions in vying for the project. It often happens that companies from the same country join rival international coalitions and compete with one another.

It is difficult however for the Japanese, with their long-ingrained habits of thinking, to develop a flair for these modes of relating to others. For me personally, it is only after many years of working in international business that I have acquired this skill. It does appear, nevertheless, that Japan is gradually making the transition to horizontal indicators. Even major corporations such as Mitsui, Mitsubishi, Sumitomo, and other so-called *keiretsu* conglomerate groups which have traditionally been characterized by hierarchical relations running down from a manufacturer or distributor at the top, are becoming less concerned with these vertical structures. The trend away from status markers is visible in fashion as well: women are now free to choose what to wear when walking around town, and you no longer see types of clothing associated with the "privileged class."

Recently I heard a rather amusing story. In an episode of the popular TV cartoon series *Sazae-san*, the main character's father was checking out bamboo brooms at the supermarket, and was mistaken for a cleaning man, which enraged him. After the scene was aired, emails and phone calls of protest came pouring in from all over the country asking program producers to stop belittling those in the cleaning profession, and demanding to know what was wrong with being a "cleaning man". This incident made me realize that Japan has shifted to more horizontal forms of social relationships since the

---

[1] *Keiretsu* literally means "system", and is a set of companies with interlocking business relationships and shareholdings. The *keiretsu* maintained dominance over the Japanese economy for the last half of the 20th century.

years that *Sazae-san* depicts.

3) From hard to soft power

Soft power, a concept advocated by Joseph Nye, a prominent international relations scholar and former dean of Harvard's Kennedy School of Government, has been adopted into US foreign policy. According to Nye, soft power is a nation's ability to build its image as a trustworthy partner and enhance its international assertiveness through attractive culture, values and government policies, as opposed to military force, economic coercion and other forms of hard power.

I completely agree with this view, which holds true for more than just foreign policy objectives. The global era is one in which actors compete on knowledge industries, intelligence that adds value to information, accumulated human wisdom, and next-generation models.

Japan has renounced war in its constitution and does not have nuclear weapons. Its sole option therefore is continuing to strengthen its soft power. Japan's foreign policy towards China in many ways is a battle between hard and soft power. China's policy towards Japan rests almost entirely on hard power approaches, including continued military expansion, the instigation of anti-Japanese riots, and recourse to military intimidation in the dispute over the Senkaku Islands. However, although Japan does need a strong national defense, attempting to contain China using hard power would be meaningless. Japan instead needs to use the tools available to free nations such as the rule of law, fair competition, and democracy and to ensure that the claims it makes in the international arena are ethically based. Activities such as contributions to international organizations and technology transfers to other countries can also help Japan expand its circle of allies.

4) The simultaneous introduction of opposite values

This is what thinking with a matrix is all about. The well-known phrase "think globally, act locally" perfectly illustrates the process of using two axes displaying different sets of values at the same time. Later, we will examine in more detail this way of reasoning, which tends to be difficult for the Japanese to master.

5) Unification of international codes and regulations

Global standards are internationally integrated standards, codes, and regulations that have developed along with the global market with the aim to overcome discrimination and disparities among firms from different countries.

However, it seems that many Japanese remain unaware of the importance of standardized regulations as a characteristic of the global era. In fact, many reject standardized regulations. For example, at a lecture recently one participant objected against global standards, on the grounds that they were in reality no more than American standards. Such comments are unfortunately not exceptional; they are part of a trend that is not just regrettable, but also dangerous. The global regulatory integration means that violations will be punished all the more severely. Failure to understand this and the continuation of business as usual, focusing primarily on customers and interpersonal relationships in disregard of regulations, are bound to eventually produce a backlash.

In January of 2012, it was reported that Yazaki Corporation and DENSO Corporation were ordered to pay fines totaling roughly 41.9 billion Japanese yen for violating US antitrust laws, and Yazaki executives were sentenced to imprisonment for up to two years. These are typical examples of the consequences of noncompliance with global regulations. Not only antitrust law violations, but also what is seen as unfair business practice may escalate into chain reactions of astronomical fines being imposed in the US, Japan, and the EU.

I once heard the comments of a young employee from a Japanese financial company which had agreed to pay a fine of 10 billion yen in the US to reach a settlement. He noted that other companies were engaging in the same practices – in other words, it was because of bad luck that his firm had been targeted – and expressed satisfaction that a settlement had been reached. This deluded way of thinking is unacceptable in a global age, and it is extremely foolhardy for companies to send such employees with little to no understanding of global business rules overseas.

6) The principle of inclusion

Another characteristic of the global era is that it clears away previously existing barriers, allowing the whole picture to appear instead. For this to be possible, one needs, as Percy Barnevik observed, an "exceptionally open mind." A notable feature of the Japanese, however, is their "power of exclusion" – although not as extreme as that of certain fellow Muslims who hate and kill each other merely because they belong to different sects. While discrimination against foreigners in Japan is notorious, more subtle, less visible forms of discrimination are still pervasive. Even participants in academic conferences and university courses that call themselves "global," are not necessarily globally aware. The principle of inclusion is the foundation of modes of living that embrace diversity, guided by a vision of humanity as one diverse global family. Such modes of living are necessary in a global age.

7) Knowledge workers

Nowadays, businesses are seeking more than just workers who perform the tasks they have been assigned. Rather, they aim to attract individuals who have the ability to add the greatest value to information, creators of next-generation models that can change our everyday lives, thinkers like Bill Gates or the late Steve Jobs. Unfortunately, this kind of talent cannot be cultivated through the same management practices of carefully circumscribing and controlling which have proved efficient on the manufacturing shop floor. Instead, what is necessary in order to produce global knowledge workers is an education methodology that prioritizes the sharing of important information and allows the greatest possible free space for new ideas and creativity.

8) Market principles and humanitarian guiding principles

Looking back at the period since the dawn of the global era, one sees that two new business models have emerged and are currently in use. The first is a model based on market principles, ensuring that businesses from any country in the world can compete fairly in the global marketplace. The second is a social business model that aims to contribute to society by targeting BOP (Base or Bottom of Pyramid: the world's poor socio-economic group). The latter is a new, rapidly expanding business model, which operates on anti-market principles, providing a positive impact through advancements in corporate social responsibility, or CSR (the social contributions of businesses otherwise conforming to market principles). Japanese companies are expected to become able to effectively deploy these two models.

TWENTY-TWO YEARS AGO, BARNEVIK WAS RIGHT ABOUT GLOBALIZATION

The logic of global business and global talent that Percy Barnevik, the former CEO of the ABB Group, advocated over two decades ago undergirds the two models mentioned above. While I have built upon his theory based on my own experience, the current relevance of his ideas is astonishing.

As described by Barnevik, global business combines the following elements.

1) **Framework** (a local-global matrix) – A global business is a world-scale federation of local companies firmly rooted in domestic markets overseen by a global control tower.
2) **Soft power** (coexistence of opposite values) – A global business belongs to all major countries, while at the same time belonging to none. It is both a small- and large-scale organization.
3) **Functions** – Its functions encompass both centralization, given the need for unified reporting and control, and extreme decentralization.
4) **Management** (maximizing and optimizing performance at the national level) – Four to six times a year, the board of directors formulates a global strategy, monitors performance, and proposes solutions for major problems. Accuracy can be sacrificed to some degree in emphasizing speed.
5) **Personnel** (both local staff and global managers at the top levels)
6) **Optimal timing of growth** (careful consideration given to the timing of trans-border mergers and acquisitions)

In order to put this vision into practice, the following are essential:

1) Top-level leadership
2) A global perspective
3) The establishment of a global strategy office (control tower)
4) Global strategy development

However, over two decades later, very few Japanese businesses have successfully developed in these areas.

Furthermore, according to Barnevik, global managers should meet the following conditions:

1) Have exceptionally open minds.
2) Respect how different countries do things, and have the imagination to appreciate why they do them that way.
3) Be adept at the same time at pushing the limits of culture and creating opportunities for innovation.
4) Show generosity and patience in handling language barriers.

These conditions for global managers are even more important today. Barnevik likely developed them as a result of his travels around the world, and of his repeated, tireless interactions with local staff. If the ABB Group was able to become a genuinely global business, it was because it created a system in which global managers who satisfied these conditions were in charge of highly capable staff worldwide.

THE IMPORTANCE OF MATRIX THINKING

Here again, I would like to emphasize the importance of matrix thinking.

The matrix is the combination of a framework with soft power; it is the co-existence of opposite values. One needs to master the habit of thinking with a local-global matrix.

A matrix holds simultaneously in sight two axes that display opposite values. It therefore enables forms of thought and behavior that allow conflicting values to coexist. In my view, basing total optimization decisions on a matrix is the type of thinking best suited for a global era.

Up until now, perceiving values in terms of binary opposites has been the norm. Only one of the options was correct, and finding the solution meant choosing the correct option. Selecting the other option was considered either incorrect or of inferior value. However, such binary thinking has the effect of dividing people, provoking hostility among them. It is indeed this kind of binary thinking that brings into being societies whose members discriminate and are discriminated against on the basis of innate attributes beyond their control.

Having a global, bird's eye view of the world means considering the Earth as a whole, free from discrimination and national borders. For this to be possible, it is imperative to cultivate ideas and actions informed by a matrix, with its simultaneous use of axes displaying diametrically opposed values. Matrix thinking makes it possible to identify the underlying causes of the accumulating global issues, and restructure the world into a more equitable place.

THE JAPANESE MISUNDERSTANDING OF WHAT CONSTITUTES GLOBAL TALENT

For some reason, a profound misunderstanding of the conditions of globalization and global talent is being perpetuated among the Japanese. A survey about the skills required of global talent was distributed to 500 staff members at five major Japanese corporations. Respondents were in their 30s and 40s, and included both individuals who already had experience working overseas, as well as staff who expected to be assigned to overseas positions in the future. Answers to this survey were gathered before staff participated in my global business seminars.

The most common type of response mentioned only English proficiency. This reveals a serious misconception since, if that were the case, then anyone whose mother tongue is English would qualify as global talent. In fact, 40% of participants considered English or other language skills necessary. Another popular response was "communication skills," which also surpassed the 40% mark. The importance of communication skills, however, is premised on the content that is being debated, on the answers given to the question, "What should we do in the global market?" Other responses of note were "familiarity with local markets, business practices and cultures," indicating the failure of the Japanese to grasp the difference between *international* and *global* business.

A professional working in global business needs the skill to pursue an understanding that is simultaneously in line with the rule axis (of global standards, etc.) and the diversity axis (of market realities), while producing fast results that ensure total optimization. In other words, the most fundamental competency necessary in global business concerns the ability to use matrix thinking in order to orient one's behavior towards total optimization. Communication skills and English proficiency are no more than means to achieving this end.

Of the 500 participants surveyed, only 5 gave answers that suggested they really understood globalization. The following are excerpts from their responses.

1) [Global business professionals] clearly understand the principles and rules for doing business in the global market, and handle situations according to the context of the particular country or region in which they operate.
2) They are adept at finding optimal solutions by integrating elements that need to be standardized and harmonized with context-specific needs. They are able to explain this way of thinking logically and persuasively.

Among these 500 staff members from five major Japanese corporations, who were either in charge of handling business with overseas partners or getting ready to be stationed overseas, only five had a correct understanding of what makes global talent. We can surmise from these results that the rest of the staff held similar views.

As a side note, the tendency in the West is to first seek a liberal arts education at a four-year university as a means to develop a holistic, diversified foundation for one's future professional life, followed for example by business school in order to acquire the knowledge necessary for managing and adding value to projects, using numerical data to gain information about a region, and crafting sales strategies. This educational model stands in stark contrast to the skills sought after in Japan. Today, effective performance in global business requires much more than business expertise. Not only for the business men and women of the current global era, but also for young people about to enter the workforce, for children, for those yet to be born – indeed for all – it is important to become well equipped to live as global citizens in a global age.

How are we going to achieve this?

I suggest that the solution lies in the experience of *navigating* five Paths. Starting with the next chapter, we will take up each of these Paths, as key elements of the art of surviving and thriving in the global age.

CHAPTER 5
CULTIVATING A GLOBAL MIND (THE FIRST PATH)

SOME MISTAKEN ASSUMPTIONS, BIG AND SMALL

I realized two things during the twenty-five years I spent doing business overseas. The first is that rumors circulating overseas about the misunderstandings the Japanese entertain are true. The second is that, if the Japanese want to gain recognition in the world, they should learn to valorize their own cultural DNA (the latter point will be covered in Chapter 8).

What I call "the misunderstandings of the Japanese" range from minor differences of opinion to serious misunderstandings that can impact Japan's future. During my time in America, I continued to subscribe to the *Nikkei Shimbun*, Japan's leading financial newspaper. I would cut out important news articles, arrange them by country and industry, and paste them into scrapbooks. I believe it was in the New Year's issue of the *Nikkei* during the third year of the Gulf War that representatives of various Japanese industries were questioned about their views of the war. Reading their responses from the perspective of someone based in the US, I found myself agreeing only with Sadako Ogata's comments. Former United Nations High Commissioner for Refugees, Sadako Ogata was at the time President of the Japan International Cooperation Agency (JICA). None of the other viewpoints expressed in the interviews, I felt, would have been acceptable to the international community. In her remarks, Ogata gave thoughtful consideration to the global situation and the diversity of positions on the issue of the war, drawing on her rich experience, which had included work in refugee areas. The rest of the comments were mere conjectures that relied heavily on scanty information from the Japanese media.

A more recent example of a Japanese misunderstanding can be found in an article titled "On the Dismantling of Ever-Growing Megabanks," in an August 2012 issue of the Japanese newspaper *Sankei Shimbun*. In this article, New York-based senior columnist Hajime Matsuura points out that in the US it is increasingly argued that the repeal of the Glass-Steagall Act, which separated banks and securities, has spawned conflicts of interests with clients, fostering corruption in major financial institutions. In Japan, however, there is a trend towards relaxing regulations on bank investments into business firms. As the rest of the world is moving in the opposite direction, Japan's case appears anachronistic.

WHILE THE WORLD MOVES FORWARD, JAPAN IS HEADING IN THE OPPOSITE DIRECTION

It is quite often the case that crucial information about the world is not transmitted to Japan in real time, losing its impact as a result. There are countless examples of this delay.

1) In 1995, the Technical Barriers to Trade (TBT) Agreement entered into force following the establishment of the World Trade Organization (WTO), with the aim to prevent discrimination in trade. It was followed later by the introduction of ISO standards. These developments led to the emergence of an integrated global market. It was a remarkable transformation that demanded, in its turn, a shift towards standardization strategies focusing simultaneously on products and standards. However, since many Japanese corporations failed to realize the

significance of these processes, it took them a while to adapt to the new conditions.

2) By the time I returned to Japan, environmentalism was on the rise across the country. What was interesting was that almost everyone believed global warming was caused by CO_2 emissions. In the US, rumors were already spreading that the basic data supporting this conclusion had been fabricated. The United Nations (UN) and NASA finally confirmed these rumors in 2009. Nonetheless, former Japanese Prime Minister Yukio Hatoyama spoke confidently at the UN of Japan's goal to cut CO_2 emissions by 25 percent.

3) Corporate social responsibility (CSR) was also popular in Japan when I returned. Following the awarding of the Nobel Peace Prize in 2006 to Muhammad Yunus for his pioneering work with the Grameen Bank, public interest in social business soared. Because of this timing, CSR and social business are often discussed in the same context in Japan. But these two phenomena stemmed from completely different trends, and actually occurred in the opposite chronological order.

Muhammad Yunus is a fellow member of Ashoka, a network that helps social entrepreneurs worldwide develop their visions into enterprises. Ashoka started in the early 1980s in the US as a new type of social change NGO. It is based on a new business model that targets the poor, relying on what might be called "anti-market principles" to effect global change. On the other hand, CSR gained momentum in the late 1990s as an approach for improving corporate practices otherwise guided by market principles. It is clear, therefore, that both the order in which these two movements were introduced and their significance are clearly different from how they are presented in Japan.

4) Little knowledge of the so-called WikiLeaks incidents. WikiLeaks, which have received in Japan even less media attention than domestic celebrity scandals, are actually of tremendous consequence, demonstrating that states no longer enjoy a monopoly of control over information. The Japanese government realized the dangers posed by WikiLeaks only after the US government announced it was revamping its national security policies.

5) Japanese corporations still place a strong emphasis on character when recruiting staff. Instead, they should attach importance to intelligence, making use of the global scales that are available for measuring aptitudes such as logical thinking in ways similar to the Grade Point Average (GPA). This is precisely the topic that writer and journalist Ken Mori addresses in his article "Recruiting at Top Corporations Switches from Character to Intelligence," published in the Japanese weekly magazine *Shukan Bunshun* on January 24, 2013). Mori finds a significant lag between Japanese employment criteria and global trends.

In Japan there is a great deal of freedom to write without fear of censorship. As a result, media of all kinds are flourishing, and important publications can be swiftly translated into Japanese. Not only are the Japanese able to travel freely overseas, but there are also large numbers of foreigners living in and visiting Japan. So why does Japan appear oblivious to the dramatic changes sweeping the world today? Why does it fail to grasp their significance?

FIVE PATHS TO BECOMING A TRUE GLOBAL PROFESSIONAL

Let's chase away the haze that prevents the Japanese from seeing those changes, using a bird's eye view to observe the world as a whole. At this point, I would like to introduce a methodology that can empower the Japanese to become true global professionals, while remaining firmly grounded in Japan's characteristic sense of values. This methodology comprises five distinct Paths.

Why use the term "Path"? The Japanese word *michi*, or, in its alternative reading, *dō*, which can be literally translated as "path" or "method," appears in the names of traditions such as *budō* ("martial arts"), *sadō* ("the tea ceremony") or *jūdō* (lit. "the gentle path"). It denotes the sustained effort required in any quest for a higher level of mastery. An individual who strives for global awareness and the great power that it affords in today's world is on a similar quest. He or she is a follower of the "global Path".

Put simply, the methodology we will discuss aims to alter approaches to learning based on a proper definition. To refine tradition and incorporate it into learning methods for the twenty-first century.

The five Paths are:

The First Path: Cultivating a global mind
The Second Path: Committing to a bird's eye view of the world, facilitated by the World Cultural Map)
The Third Path: Training an ethical and legal mind
The Fourth Path: Refining Japanese cultural DNA to develop Japanese-style

global talent

The Fifth Path: Transitioning to twenty-first-century approaches to learning

In what follows, we will discuss, in order, each of these Paths. For the rest of this chapter we will consider the First Path: a global mind.

THE MOST FUNDAMENTAL THING OF ALL: HAVING A GLOBAL MIND

The first task toward which we should direct our efforts is understanding that a global mind is the key foundation for living and opening up new opportunities in the global age.

I heard the following story from an individual who had recently returned from Russia. Apparently Japanese staff working at the Russian office of a major Japanese auto manufacturer tended to treat Russians with condescension, which was obviously upsetting to the locals. Hearing this story brought back memories of a similar sight I had witnessed at ASEAN events. My heart ached as I thought, "the Japanese haven't changed at all".

The roots of these attitudes can be found in the Japanese conviction that declining domestic demand is to be offset by moving business to Russia or other Asian countries. However, nowadays individuals and businesses from all countries find themselves, from the start, on an equal footing in a global playing field, where they must compete promptly and decisively under fair rules. **Given such conditions, the Japanese cannot win against the competition if they treat people from other countries in a discriminatory fashion.**

A few years ago I visited the California branch office of a Japanese mega-bank, only to be terribly disappointed. I was unable to see the courteous Japanese-style service, based on the principle that "the client is god," as it is often said in Japan. The reception at the teller's window was no different from that at other local banks. Perhaps bank staff thought that, since American banks tend to offer lackluster service, they needed to follow suit. But in a global playing field, staff at Japanese banks should provide the same high-quality customer service in America as they do at home. Globalization does not mean merely conforming to local ways of doing things.

USING THE MIND'S EYE

A global mind engages the world in its entirety; its scale is such that it can hold within its embrace the whole of reality. It sees all people as equal beings, endowed with both their own cultural DNA and basic human rights (innate rights which must be guaranteed to each person by virtue of being human). This awareness lies at the foundation of a global mind.

To describe the global mind, I often draw on Buddhist teachings, from the Zen concept of "mind's eye" to the *Heart Sutra*. Using the mind's eye is important since the world is only partially visible to the physical eye. On the other hand, the idea of a globalized world as an "interconnected whole" resonates with the way in which the world is envisioned in the *Heart Sutra*.

Alternatively, we can attempt a different explanation. The Japanese, being born, raised, educated, and employed in Japan, are unaware that they cultivate a mind with just enough capacity to accommodate the Japanese reality: a mind the size of Japan. This is why even when important global information reaches Japan, the Japanese are seldom able to comprehend its significance. A global mind that can hold the entire world in its embrace – a mind-vessel of the largest possible capacity – needs to be nurtured from a young age.

This is not to say that one cannot successfully develop a global mind as an adult. The key is to completely revise one's approach to learning. We will consider this problem in more detail when we discuss the Fifth Path.

In his book, *The World is Flat 3.0*, published in 2005, American journalist and three-time Pulitzer Prize winner Thomas Friedman posits that the world has entered a new era marked by dramatic changes comparable in magnitude to those of the industrial revolution. According to Friedman this shift happened around the year 2000. This shift caused people worldwide to realize that they had more power than ever to act globally as *individuals*.

By becoming more global as individuals, the Japanese can also tap into this tremendous power.

SEVEN THOUGHT PATTERNS FOR BEING GLOBALLY COMPETITIVE

Once you have successfully built the vast receptacle of a global mind, it is important to be self-conscious about the thought patterns you fill it with. It was on the pursuit of this issue that I staked the survival of my company, as I competed with world-renowned business schools and brand-name training companies operating on a large scale.

I have chosen seven thought patterns: five are shared by people from different cultural backgrounds, and two are particularly relevant for the Japanese.

These thought patterns are helpful when seeking to have a persuasive impact on people from different cultures, or when proposing ideas that diverge from their expectations.

The seven thought patterns are:
1. A bird's eye view perspective;
2. The ability to be simultaneously aware of the specificity of the current setting and of the largest possible scope on the space axis (the world) and time axis (5000 years);
3. Discernment that extends beyond the immediately visible to grasp mega-trends and formulate strategic visions;
4. A multicultural lens;
5. Oscillating between *macro* and *micro* perspectives.

The two thought patterns that I consider especially relevant for the Japanese are:
6. The ability to use words, diagrams, and models for strong, effective communication, and
7. Speed

Let us look at these seven thought patterns in order.

1. A bird's eye view perspective

An overall or bird's eye view perspective of the world is the most important new skill for the global age. Without a firm grasp of the entire playing field of competition, it is impossible to be truly strategic. Knowledge of the whole picture is therefore a prerequisite for designing a strategy.

A good example that illustrates this point is former Malaysian Prime Minister Mahathir bin Mohamad's contribution to the creation of the Association of Southeast Asian Nations (ASEAN) in order to protect Southeast Asian countries from the menace of communism. When, in December 1990, Mahathir bin Mohamad proposed the formation of an East Asian Economic Group (EAEG), he acted in accordance with a bird's eye view of the world. He understood that, if East Asia was to maintain its unique identity, countries in this region needed to work together. While EAEG encountered opposition from the US and its allies, the current success of ASEAN would not have been possible without Mahathir bin Mohamad's remarkable insight.

Those whose perspective, originating in Japan, is limited to a specific country become completely divorced from global strategy. All too often, Japanese executives and HR managers send new employees overseas trusting that they will naturally metamorphose into global talent. Such corporate leaders tend to leave concerns about global strategy into the hands of foreign staff, believing that there is no need for their Japanese employees to develop strategic thinking.

Having a bird's eye view is also related to the seventh pattern, speed, which we will look at later. Those who have internalized the bird's eye view typically are quick to take action to reach their objectives. They tend to rely less on vertical indicators, while horizontal relationships – interpersonal bonds, solidarity, and alliances - become more important.

For corporations, a bird's eye view can be extremely helpful in identifying optimal markets, choosing locations for factories and research and development centers, exporting from specific countries in order to avoid tariffs, or determining if pricing is discriminatory towards certain countries and customers. It also has the advantage of making it possible to discern distortions in the global distribution of wealth and resources and to have a greater awareness of humanitarian issues.

Carlos Ghosn, Chairman and CEO of the Renault-Nissan Alliance, who spent his early childhood in Lebanon and his school years in Europe before becoming a corporate CEO in the US, clearly had a talent for observing the world from a bird's eye view. Ghosn transformed Nissan's headquarters into global headquarters and created a Western-style risk management department, using a bird's eye view to develop strategies that led to Nissan's spectacular turnaround as a major automobile manufacturer.

A bird's eye view creates a sense of constantly observing oneself from a distance. This perspective, known as risk management, is an essential skill in an age of increasing global risk.

2. The ability to be simultaneously aware of the specificity of the current setting and of the largest possible scope on the space axis (the world) and time axis (5000 years)

One feature that distinguishes the Japanese from citizens of other nations is their relatively weak awareness of spatial and temporal scales. A large percentage of the world's population follows monotheistic religions: Judaism, Christianity, Islam. From an early age, monotheistic faiths instill an awareness of large spatial and temporal scales encompassing concepts of heaven, hell, and a day of final judgment. Later, in college, these individuals study religious thought and classical literature along these axes, as liberal arts. This education equips them to grasp large scales of space and time better than their Japanese counterparts, even though the content of their studies may have been otherwise similar.

Japan's sometimes "difficult" Chinese neighbors consider that their history spans a period of over 5000 years. Thus, thought patterns based on an axes system covering large temporal and spatial scales are wired into the Chinese cultural DNA. Previously, a US Trade Department Representative urged the Chinese government to increase penalties for intellectual property rights violations. The Chinese government objected, arguing that China had created Chinese characters and the compass, among numerous other inventions that are freely used by people all over the world without paying patent fees. Such logic demonstrates the scales of space and time that the Chinese people naturally operate with.

In contrast, the Japanese "field-oriented" approach is in one sense the effect of a limited awareness of spatial and temporal scales. But there is no need to reject this way of thinking. The key is to continue to tap into the explosive force of the present setting, while allowing one's mind to be configured by the world as the ultimate scale on the spatial axis, and the past 5000 years as the time axis. Matrix thinking can serve both as inspiration for original, value-added product development, and as resource for debates at international conferences.

3. Discernment that extends beyond the immediately visible to grasp megatrends and formulate strategic visions

Next in importance in the repertoire of thought patterns for the global era is a visionary faculty that extends beyond the immediately visible, allowing one to detect megatrends.

Put simply, it means exercising this visionary power to extract certain laws from the accumulated history of humankind. These laws are then applied to the future, as a technique for predicting what will happen if immediate action is not taken. For example, the book *Megachange: The World in 2050* (2012. Profile Books, Ltd.), penned by the editorial team at *The Economist*, and which received a great deal of public attention, makes the claim that religion will slowly fade away. This prediction is an instantiation of the kind of discernment required to grasp megatrends.

In addition to understanding the megatrends that shape the global era, it is important to consistently and accurately convey one's own strategic vision, be it personal or organizational. In this regard, Hitachi is one of the rare Japanese corporations to put forward a message that indicates both a firm grasp of megatrends and a specific business strategy:

social innovation = social infrastructure + IT

Multicultural lens

Learning to view Japan and the Japanese from the other's perspective

Indicators

	Single lens	Multicultural lens
Indivisual	• A false notion that your values and business practices are the only right ones • Narrow vision • Biased interpretation • Lack of flexibility • Limited, rigid solutions	• Openness to a diversity of values and business practices, to be drawn on as needed in pursuit of desired goals. • Broad vision • Balanced interpretation • High flexibility • Broad range of available solutions
Inter-personal	• Low tolerance • Suppression of others' creative thinking • Proneness to negotiation failure • Difficulty of team cooperation • Inability to appreciate others' talents	• High tolerance • Stimulation of others' creative thinking • An enabling environment for win-win ideas, coupled with high potential for negotiation success • Team cooperation producing synergy effects • Appreciation of others' talents

4. A multicultural lens

One of the biggest reasons why the Japanese struggle with misunderstanding is that they peer at the outside world through a window from inside Japan. They conspicuously lack the ability to view Japan and the Japanese people from an outside perspective.

This situation is symbolically summed up in one question the Japanese media tend to pose to foreign visitors: "What do you think Japan should do?" The logic implicit in this question is that "we ourselves view the world through a single lens." This is one of the practices that I find terribly embarrassing, along with other typically Japanese customs, such as apologizing when you have done nothing wrong or laughing for no reason.

Here, I use the term "lens" to refer to a *cultural lens*. The ability to switch perspectives by "putting oneself in the other person's shoes" is highly valued in Japan. Using a multicultural lens to achieve mutual understanding involves a similarly de-centered procedure of perspective-taking, whereby one learns to alternate between one's own and the other's cultural lens, and even to see through both lenses at the same time.

It is important to emphasize here that I am not simply advocating a *dual-country* lens. I was once invited to a seminar held by a Japanese businessman very experienced in doing business in China. His words had the persuasive power that comes from abundant, first-hand experience. And yet, since his discussion was framed only by the two cultural lenses of Japan and China, it struck me with a sense of incongruity. With a multicultural lens, it is possible to make adjustments and communicate from a higher perspective.

In practice, international communication and negotiations often go awry due to a failure to use a multicultural lens. I myself have experienced difficulties in negotiations with HR managers, when running global seminars at multinational corporations headquartered in the US or China. These difficulties arose from the fact that, even though these HR managers belonged to multinational corporations, many of them had never worked abroad, and therefore could only focus on the position of their local employees.

Whenever this happened, I relied on tools such as the Cultural World Map, approaching the problem from a higher perspective in order to persuade my interlocutors and gain their acceptance.

If the Japanese are to learn how to use a multicultural lens, global education from a young age is of utmost importance. I also recommend that adults use study tools such as the Cultural World Map and the Global Navigator, which we will discuss later. In particular, knowing what local people value, both positively and negatively, is a shortcut for understanding their cultural lens.

When it comes to using a multicultural lens, the Japanese have an advantage. At the seminars I taught in different places around the world, I have oftentimes encountered participants who said they were glad I was not an American instructor. Apparently, not being an American is associated with a better command of a multicultural lens.

5. Oscillating between macro and micro perspectives

Using both a macro and a micro perspective to address a particular issue will instantly boost the persuasive power of an explanation. This is a powerful skill for impressing and convincing those who come from different cultures. In discussions about global environmental issues, for instance, backing your ideas with concrete data about the amount of waste that Tokyo produces daily and how this is processed will greatly increase your powers of persuasion.

Another example is the Internet. When viewed from a micro (local) level, the Internet is free, convenient – indeed the positives are endless. From a macro (global) level, however, it becomes evident that American IT companies are receiving the greatest gains. Grounding ideas about how to do business in these complementary viewpoints makes it possible to propose more convincing business models.

These perspectives are fundamental to traditional Japanese arts, collectively referred to as *dō* ("paths," or "ways), such as flower arrangement (*kadō*) or the tea ceremony (*sadō*). In Japanese flower arrangement, one cuts tree branches and flower stems, and then anchors them on a metal pin holder (*kenzan*). What is visible to the naked eye is the arrangement of flowers; what the mind's eye contemplates is an expanded reflection of the natural world. In *sadō,* participants sip tea in a small tearoom, with the sound of water boiling in the background, an aesthetic and spiritual practice that promotes a heightened awareness of the workings of the universe, transcending the five senses. As I ponder on such aspects, I am once again amazed at the depth of meaning revealed in these arts, which build on elements of Eastern philosophy. An incursion into the world of Japan's traditional arts suggests that the Japanese are far from unfamiliar with balancing macro and micro perspectives.

Allowing one's thinking to travel back and forth between a macro and a micro perspective is beneficial in yet another way. The ability to quickly oscillate between the two makes it possible to free oneself of conventional thinking (cleansing the mind of its habits and attachments) in order to attain dynamic, intrinsic and profound understanding and inspiration.

The five thought patterns we have discussed so far are universally sought after in the global age. The following is an example of applying these thought patterns. An ombudsman group in New Jersey showed an interest in my global education program for children, "Ten Steps to Reach the Global

Village", and recommended introducing it in schools. However, one ombudsman member commented that a PhD was required in order to teach in US schools.

I explained that, although I did not have a PhD, I had earned tenured professorship, and I could have it officially recognized by a specialized institution as equivalent to a doctoral degree. At the same time, I posed the following question: "Are we failing to realize the more important issue here? Asian values are included in global education as well. In Eastern traditions, students learned from "masters" (*shi*), individuals who had become accomplished in their respective "paths." The PhD degree is a modern, Euro-American institution. Isn't the idea that only PhD holders can teach global education extremely limiting – even anti-global?"

Everyone fell silent, and the group leader mumbled quietly that I brought up a valid point. It didn't take long for the program to be enthusiastically adopted.

6. The ability to use words, diagrams, and models for strong, effective communication

The two thought patterns we discuss below are particularly necessary for the Japanese. I previously referenced a survey asking 500 staff members in major Japanese corporations what abilities were required to perform as global staff, which showed that over 40% of respondents considered English or other foreign language skills important.

It goes without saying that language proficiency is important in global business. Nevertheless, on the subject of language proficiency, an episode comes to mind of an HR manager at a well-known Japanese corporation where I conducted a training program.

This HR manager was slated to be transferred to ASEAN, so I recommended that he participate in global business coaching or seminars. He flatly refused. The reason he gave for his refusal was that he already had decent TOEIC (Test of English for International Communication) scores.

I am not sure if he actually believed that being a good global manager merely meant having good English skills, or if his pride revolted at the idea of taking lessons from someone else. Either way, I later heard that this manager ended up running into difficulties communicating with local staff, which affected his performance.

To become a successful global manager one needs a powerful message that subscribes to the principles of the global age, as well as mastery of the thought patterns needed to convey this message, rather than just linguistic competence. You need content that will form the backbone of your endeavors. If Carlos Ghosn, who came from Renault to Japan to turn around the ailing Nissan, came to be considered a master of communication despite not having a strong command of the Japanese language, it was precisely because of his ability to get his message across.

Unlike some Europeans and North Americans, the Japanese are not as comfortable with using emphatic hand and body gestures to communicate. That is why I recommend using diagrams and models instead.

The Japanese have an exceptional ability to explain with diagrams. I remember the Global Strategy document of a leading Japanese corporation I worked with, which consisted of page after page of intelligently designed, exquisite diagrams. When foreign presenters are asked to use graphic explanation, their diagrams tend to be difficult to decipher. In some cases, they find themselves unable to draw a diagram and offer instead a textual narrative.

I myself relied heavily on diagrams and models in the training programs I developed during my time in the US, much to the delight of participants. One diagram that received rave reviews illustrated differences among Asia's major ethnic groups. For example, the Japanese custom of *nemawashi* – which literally means "going around the roots," referring to informal, behind-the-scene discussions that lay the groundwork for consensus building – is difficult to explain verbally to people from countries not familiar with this practice. Using a diagram that depicts the human relationships involved, however, greatly enhances the audience's ability to grasp the meaning of the concept.

Making models is also more important now than ever before. This is because models provide methods that can be followed anywhere in the world to arrive at the same results.

As values around the world underwent major transformations in the mid 1990s, past models became outdated. The question now is, who will create new models? We, the Japanese, could be the ones to do it. Now is the time where originality and model design skills are being demanded. If we can create new generation models that can change lifestyles worldwide, we will also enjoy great success in business.

I recommend using models as media of communication in cross-border debates, and thus turning these debates into opportunities to further refine one's model design skills.

What does it mean to communicate through models? Take the following example: suppose there is a large difference in productivity between a certain Asian country and a Latin American country. To understand the situation, you first compare manufacturing processes in the two countries using diagrams. If a problem is found, you try to identify a manufacturing model usable in both countries. Once the model becomes widespread, it can be considered a next-generation model. Emerging next-generation models include fully automated production using artificial intelligence and smart grid technologies.

Currently I provide training for Japanese corporations that have engaged in global mergers and acquisitions (M&As), assisting them with the post-M&A integration process. As Percy Barnevik of ABB explicitly put it, such cross-border M&As are ideal opportunities to build new global business. For example, if staff from Germany, Singapore, Japan, and the US wish to create a global team model drawing selectively on best practices from each country, an effective strategy for approaching the task is to develop country-based models that capture the nuances of the term "team" and the differences among its uses. Having virtual teams discuss how things are different and why can serve as a valuable exercise in *navigating* each country's values. Comparing models side by side in this way aids companies in creating their own global corporate model.

7. Speed

The final thought pattern we will consider here is speed. Unfortunately, Japanese companies are infamous for being slow to act. They also seem to lag in terms of responsiveness to problems. And these tendencies are becoming commonplace in their international operations as well. American global corporations such as GE and IBM and neighboring Korea's Samsung function according to an entirely different sense of speed. On several occasions, I have heard versions of the following story from staff in our client companies. Apparently, all too often, when Samsung makes business inquiries, Japanese corporations provide a delivery date so far out that those at Samsung decide to take matters in their own hands. There appear to be countless reasons for these delays, making it impossible to pinpoint any one cause. Several factors are entangled together, resulting in a rather complex issue. If I may venture an opinion, I would mention the following three issues as responsible for this phenomenon.

- An excessive preoccupation in Japanese society with interpersonal relationships;
- An assumption that consensus-based decision making is democratic and therefore correct, combined with a lack of leadership;
- A dissonance between trends in Japan and major global changes.

These problems pervade the entire Japanese society and will take time to address. Therefore, transforming individual learning methods in order to cultivate global awareness (an ample mind-vessel) and thought patterns for responding nimbly to evolving conditions anywhere in the world, may allow the shortest path to change.

CHAPTER 6
A BIRD'S EYE VIEW: THE CULTURAL WORLD MAP (THE SECOND PATH)

THE CULTURAL WORLD MAP – AN ORIGINAL TOOL FOR SHAPING A CAPACIOUS VESSEL FOR THE MIND

Once you have taught your mind to be globally aware, you are ready to examine the world from a bird's eye view. Many people, however, find themselves facing a "blank map" when their knowledge about the world's various regions is put to the test.

So what is the quickest way to gain a thorough grasp of the world? I recommend a tool that I have designed: the Cultural World Map. Of the numerous tools that I have developed over the years, it has been the most appreciated. Those who use the map applaud its usefulness, and often tell me they wish they had found it sooner. The Cultural World Map is intended to help users understand the mental make-up of various people throughout the world.

Following the collapse of the Cold War system, global business rules have become more standardized. At the same time, ethnic identity and cultural DNA have surfaced as important values. But attempting to grasp these phenomena used to be a spotty undertaking, as there were no mechanisms for approaching them. The toolkit I describe in this chapter was conceived to address that need.

CULTURAL OLYMPICS

A certain episode provided me with a significant, formative experience that gave me greater awareness of global cultural diversity. It was after graduating from college in Japan, while I was studying creative writing at the University of British Columbia in Canada.

Iowa State University is home to the renowned International Writing Program (IWP). This program invites young writers from all over the world to work together on the production of literary work. Needless to say, I desperately wanted to enter the program. Although the selection process was intense, I somehow managed to get accepted and moved to Iowa in 1976.

The campus grounds were enclosed on all sides by soybean fields, forming a vacuum-sealed cultural environment that would be unimaginable in Japan. It was here that, for the next four months, I would eat and sleep under the same roof with a group of young writers overflowing with cultural diversity and creative energy. With 23 participants from 22 countries, the program could easily be described as a "Cultural Olympics". It was this diversity that caused a number of problems during the first month. For example, in one university-sponsored outing, it emerged that the lunches provided contained ham. The discovery caused quite a stir, given the presence of two or three Muslim students, whose dietary restrictions prohibited the consumption of pork. In another instance, our American hosts had a hard time processing the fact that an Indonesian poet had no last name. Another member, a playwright from Argentina, was habitually at least an hour late to appointments, which did not seem to bother him in the slightest. A homosexual novelist from the Netherlands once attended a party together with a young man whom he had leashed like a dog. I have to admit even I was caught off guard.

These diverse participants would take turns presenting their writing, in oftentimes poor English. Two months later, everyone was exhausted by stress and emotionally unstable as a result. After all, this was only natural. Isolated from friends, family, and colleagues, severed from the society they used to call home, they suddenly found themselves inside an hermetically-sealed box, where they had to prove their talent against others, in a foreign language. Many participants developed sleeping problems due to chronic psychological stress.

As the end of the four-month program drew near, however, everyone had started to relax into the routine. On the other hand, one Argentinian writer lamented the fact that political adversaries had staged a coup d'état in her homeland, making it impossible for her to return to the career she had built in Argentina. A writer from Yugoslavia was worried about the deteriorating situation in the Balkan Peninsula. In just four months the world had experienced a multitude of changes. Getting ready to leave, I bade farewell to a friend, a poet from South Africa, saying I would keep in touch by phone. But he responded that he had no phone at home. I realized anew that there was a vast world out there that was still unknown to me. I often wonder how many of those participants are still safe and sound today.

The four months spent in Iowa added vibrant color to a world map that had so far been mostly blank for me. They were my formative experience of globalization. When I later designed the Cultural World Map, I wanted it to guide similar experiences: to help people paint colors onto the blank mental map they may have of certain regions of the world.

CLASSIFYING THE WORLD INTO FOUR BROAD CULTURAL CODES

Let's turn our attention to understanding the Cultural World Map. Its main component is the Global Navigator, which consists of an informational brochure covering 30 countries and a Bird's Eye View Map, and is accompanied by a user's manual.

Take a moment first to look at the Bird's Eye View Map on pages 104 and 105. The map presents a general overview of the world, classifying its regions according to three major codes. These three codes can be used to divide the world's seven billion people in terms of what they consider to be their core values. Thus, codes are value systems that form the basis of social rules. Numerous exceptions exist, of course, and the codes are merely tools for gaining a rough conceptual understanding of the world. Here, however, we will place less emphasis on exceptions, focusing instead on those absolutes found at the heart of culture.

CHAPTER 6　A BIRD'S EYE VIEW: THE CULTURAL WORLD MAP (THE SECOND PATH)

The Cultural World Map for the Global Era

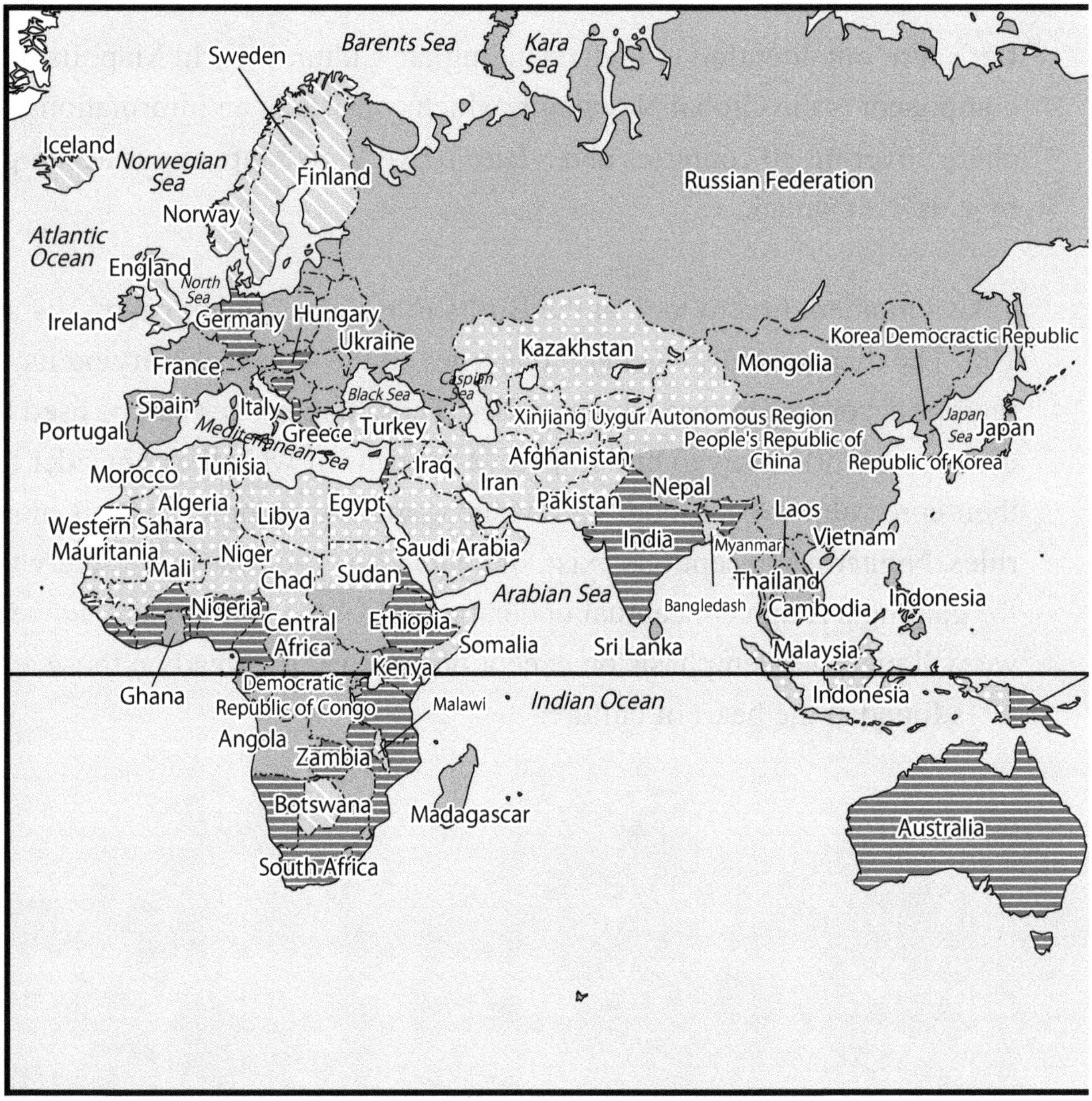

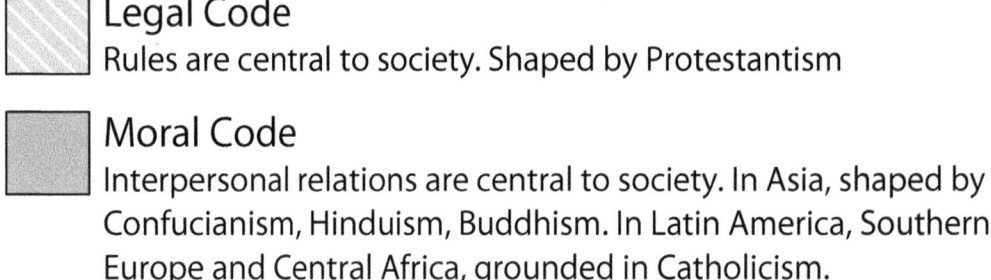

Legal Code
Rules are central to society. Shaped by Protestantism

Moral Code
Interpersonal relations are central to society. In Asia, shaped by Confucianism, Hinduism, Buddhism. In Latin America, Southern Europe and Central Africa, grounded in Catholicism.

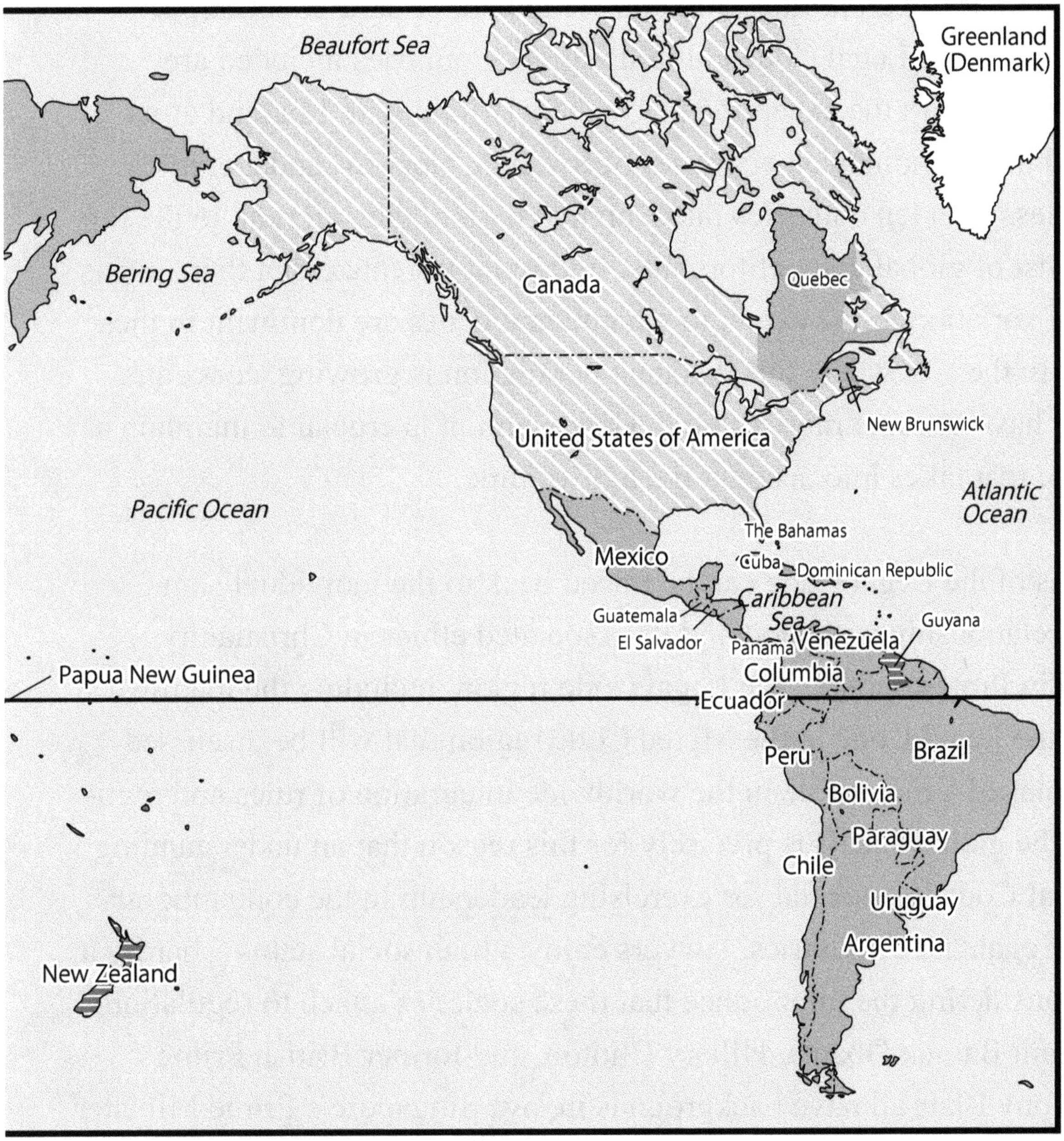

Religious Code
God's teachings are central to society. Shaped by Islam.

Mixed Code
Cultures in which salient elements of at least two of the three codes coexist.

1) The Legal Code

In the first cultural region, rules and knowledge are of paramount importance. I call this the Legal Code cultural region. Countries included are the US, Canada with the exception of Quebec, Britain with England at its center, and the Scandinavian countries of Sweden, Norway, and Denmark. Although less than ten countries make up this region, they all rank in the top 20 on the list of global competitors. It is important to realize that there exists substantial variation in the extent to which legal codes are dominant in these countries. In the US, where the Hispanic population is growing, concentration levels have become more diluted. Here again, it is crucial to maintain a perspective that takes into account the axis of time.

The origins of the Legal Code can be traced back to the individual's unmediated relationship with God and its associated ethics in Christianity, especially in Protestantism. The Legal Code region, including the manifestations of the Legal Code in the Mixed Code region that will be discussed later, has played a major role in the worldwide integration of rules and regulations in the global age. It is precisely for this reason that an understanding of the Legal Code is essential for exercising leadership in the contemporary world. In Legal Code countries, lawyers enjoy a high social status – hardly a surprise considering the importance that these societies attach to regulations. US President Barack Obama, Hillary Clinton, and former British Prime Minister Tony Blair all have backgrounds in law. Singapore's Prime Minister Lee Kuan Yew, a prominent leader in Asia, was also trained as a lawyer.

The global age demands fair competition based on standardized regulations. The skill to make this possible is a critical requirement for those who assume roles of leadership. Simply possessing good people skills is not sufficient.

2) The Moral Code

Societies that place interpersonal relationships at the core of their value systems are grouped together into the Moral Code region. These countries are characterized by a strong belief that cultivating morality and good relationships with others will lead to business success.

I often use the term "exchange of favors" when describing the specificity of this region. Alternatively, it could also be called the principle of "returning a favor." Favors are generous or helpful acts done for the benefit of others. As individuals go beyond the standard call of duty, using extra time and money to provide for others the things they want, need, or give them joy, and as these acts are then returned, a structure of reciprocation is created and relationships are reinforced. However, if you are always on the receiving end and your favor account is in substantial deficit, you may run into relationship problems.

One distinguishing characteristic of the Cultural World Map is that it lumps together Asian countries with a Confucian heritage, and Catholic regions such as Latin America, Southern Europe, and Central Africa into one Moral Code Region. To some, it may seem far-fetched to group such diverse areas together. Indeed, for a long time it was believed that the West and the East were not to be mixed. If you are uncomfortable grouping Confucian areas together with Catholic areas, feel free to divide the countries in this group into a Confucian-type Moral Code region and a Catholic-type Moral Code region. We should remember, however, that the influence of religion on society might eventually ebb away.

Some will be surprised to see former communist countries included in the

Moral Code region. This is because, with the vanishing of the Iron Curtain (or Bamboo Curtain in the case of China), it became apparent that societies like Russia or China were in many ways patriarchal societies, underneath the surface layer of political ideology. When looking at these societies in terms not of political systems, but of cultural codes, we cannot but conclude that they match the profile of the Moral Code region.

One of the major problems that Moral Code countries are confronted with is corruption. According to Transparency International's 2010 annual report, countries in this group ranked relatively low on the Corruption Perception Index (CPI), with China ranking 78, Vietnam 116, and Russia 154. On the other hand, Singapore, with former lawyer Lee Kuan Yew at its helm, topped the list as the most transparent nation in the world. Other Legal Code countries also ranked at the top. In Moral Code countries, corruption runs rampant when interpersonal relationships become linked to power. To increase transparency, it is desirable to incorporate into these systems the strong ethical values of the Legal Code. Incidentally, the CPI ranks Japan 17th.

Both the Legal Code and the Religious Code, which will be considered in the next section, attach absolute value to the laws and divine teachings at their center. In contrast, Moral Code cultures are organized around relationships, and are therefore characterized by relativity. Although rules and regulations are understood in these cultures, it is relationships that structure the conduct of business.

The Moral Code region comprises a large number of countries. To develop a more sophisticated sense of how cultural codes operate, one needs to go beyond the level of the nation-state and examine the cultural DNA of ethnic groups against one another. The Global Navigator introduced later in this chapter can facilitate this deeper understanding.

3) The Religious Code

In the Religious Code region, central values are anchored in the teachings of God. Here, divine instruction is treated as the national constitution, controlling politics, the economy, and lifestyles. In principle, this third region overlaps with the Islamic cultural sphere. Countries with Christian, Buddhist, and Hindu traditions are not included. The Religious Code region comprises the Middle East with the exception of the Mixed Code nations of Israel and Lebanon, along with Northern African countries, Pakistan, Bangladesh and other South Asian countries, as well as Southeast Asian countries such as Malaysia and Brunei. One exception is Indonesia, where Islam has not been declared the national religion, despite the fact that some 88% of the total population is Muslim. It cannot, therefore, be considered a purely Religious Code country.

At present, the Middle East and Northern Africa are gaining visibility in the global arena as new markets and resource reserves. Ethnic and religious tensions, however, have made this a troubled region, closely linked to the emergence and proliferation of international terrorist organizations. It is unfortunate that, despite the opportunities that the integration of the global market presents, this region has become so volatile.

We need to keep in mind that roughly one in four people in the world is Muslim (1.57 billion people). Faith in the same God has the rare power of creating solidarity even among people scattered in the four corners of the

CHAPTER 6 A BIRD'S EYE VIEW: THE CULTURAL WORLD MAP (THE SECOND PATH)

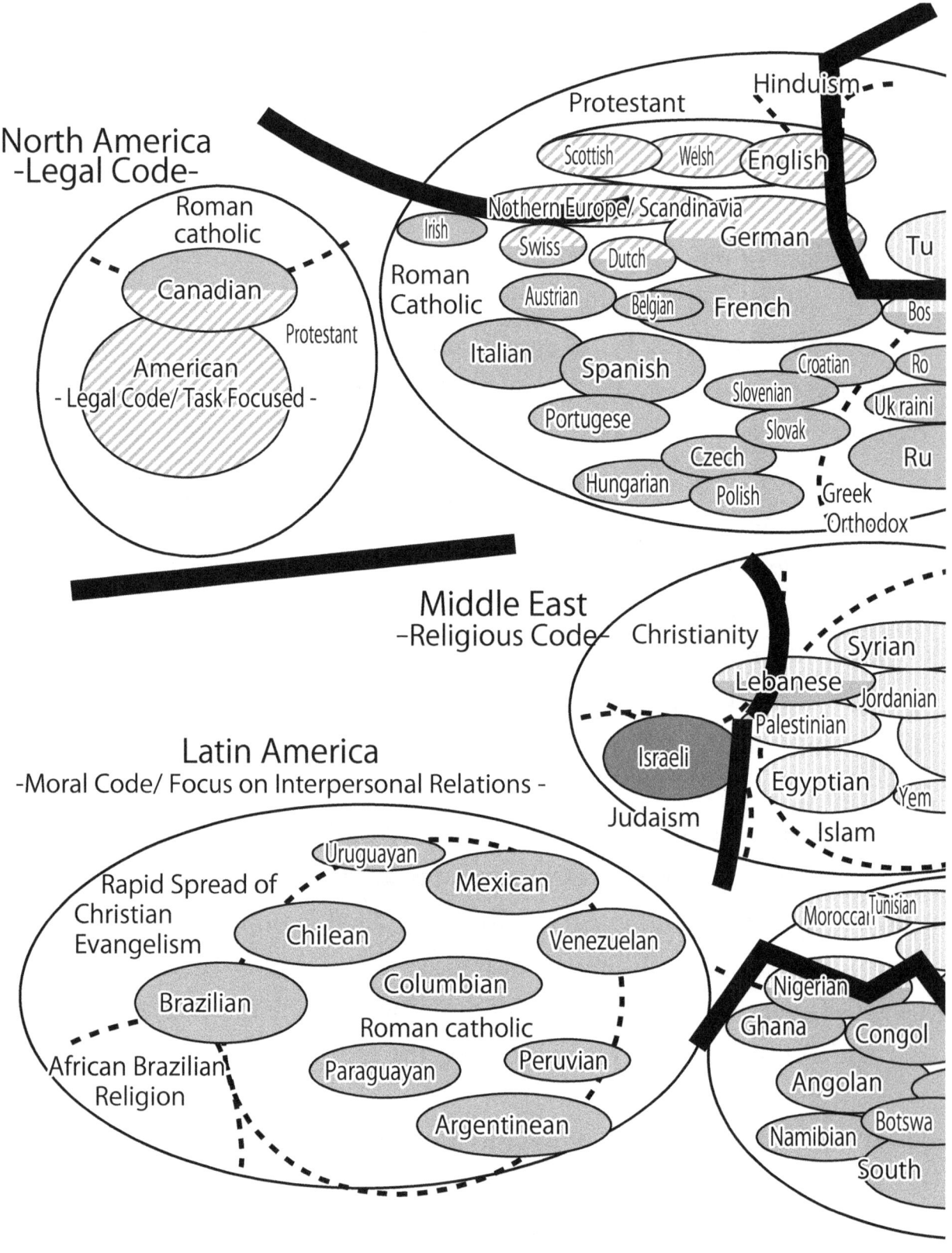

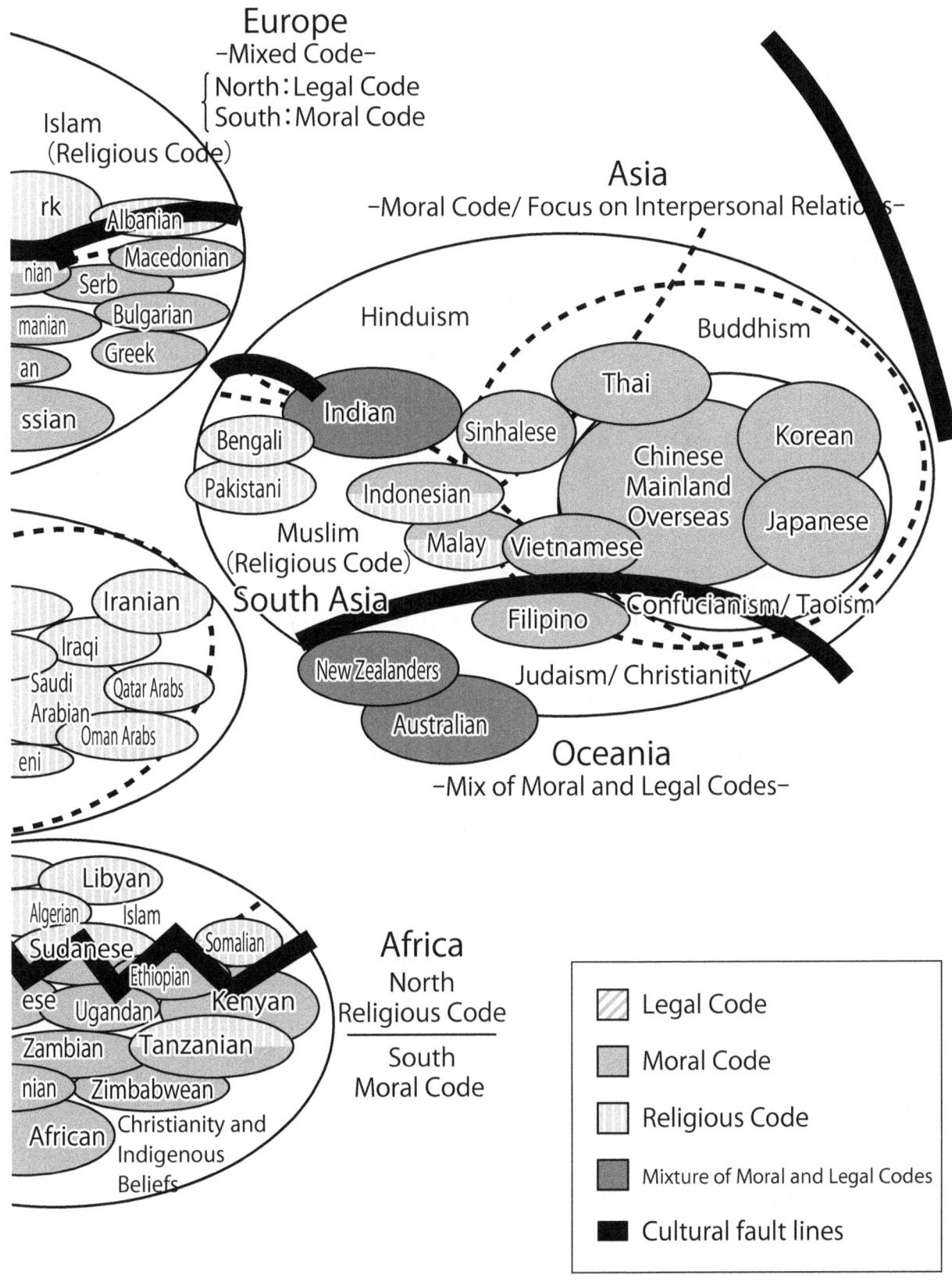

world. What is important is not to be swayed by superficial knowledge, and to cultivate a perspective of the world that can rise above ethnic and religious conflicts. Japan, whose religious thought has been less shaped by monotheism, can bring a more neutral stance to collective efforts to contain the current cycle of fear and hatred stemming from these conflicts.

4) The Mixed Code

There are geographic areas that do not fit neatly into any one of the three codes we have covered. Areas in which two of the three codes coexist are grouped together into the Mixed Code region. This hybridity is either the result of historical shifts in values, or of the presence within the same territory of different religious communities.

Some of the countries included in the Mixed Code Region are:
- Australia – a country with an ever-fluctuating identity

  Australia is not only geographically disconnected from other continents, but it is also characterized by a duality stemming from its history as a British penal colony. The country is currently transitioning from its former "White Australia Policy" to a new, ambivalent identity that oscillates between the acceptance of diverse ethnicities and cultures, on the one hand, and the rejection of refugees, on the other.
- India – Traditionally a Moral Code country, which became engrafted with elements of Legal Code while it was a British colony.
- Germany and the Netherlands – Countries with roughly equal ratios of Protestant and Catholic population. Kazakhstan, with its approximately equal ratios of Muslim, Christian, and nonreligious population can be considered similar.
- Israel – A country closely identified with an ethnic religion (Judaism)

which predates the evolution of the world religions of Christianity and Islam, and in which all the codes discussed above exist intermingled.

The overall conclusion to be drawn from our discussion so far is that it is possible to characterize the world's seven billion people in terms of four cultural codes along an axis of diversity.

The illustration on pages 110 and 111 shows how this classification can be broken down further by ethnicity. The black bold lines in between the different cultural codes represent cultural fault lines. Up until now Japanese businesses have completely ignored these cultural fault lines when venturing abroad. I am aware of a large number of problems that Japanese businesses had to face overseas over the past twenty years, most of which could have been avoided had they first taken the time to learn about local cultural codes and ways of thinking.

WHAT CAUSED THE TOYOTA RECALL CRISIS?

Before we look at several concrete examples of such failures in more depth, let us examine the conditions that led to these situations. First, the Legal and Moral Code regions are opposite worlds in almost every particular. This means that, although Japan and the United States, for instance, may be considered as relatively close, in reality they are each the reverse of the other.

I am still keenly aware of this fact despite having lived in America for twenty-five years. Actions taken with good intentions have backfired, words spoken have been taken the wrong way, time, money and energy have been wasted, astronomical fines paid, and in worst case scenarios people have been imprisoned because of differences between the US and Japan.

The Toyota recall incident in the US is a typical example. When business-related problems occur in Japan, the appropriate way to address questions in a first stage is to say that you are still collecting information and are not yet in a position to provide an opinion. After the matter has been thoroughly investigated, the concerned parties hold a press conference where they apologize profusely, with deep, deferential bows. This is considered an honest way of handling problems. Such practices do not work in the US. Instead, the CEO first comes forward by holding a press conference, and promises to spare no effort in solving the problem at hand. Top leaders need to formally take charge of the situation for an effort to solve problems to count as sincere.

Even before a fatal crash on a Californian highway led to the largest recall in Toyota's history, the company had already received numerous reports from insurance companies. But Toyota had failed to recall its cars, despite the mounting number of reports that people had been killed in accidents caused by accelerator and brake problems. Toyota's slow response led to distrust by the American public, who believed that the company was covering up major defects. Ultimately, no evidence was found to support the argument that manufacturing defects caused sudden acceleration. Nonetheless, the incident was a heavy blow to Toyota's reputation.

In yet another instance, about twenty years ago, Sumitomo Corporation relied heavily on relationships when making their sales pitch for a subway construction bid in Washington D.C. Just as it seemed that Sumitomo was going to win the bid, it was suddenly given to the competitor. Those at Sumitomo felt deeply betrayed, but they should not have expected business strategies based in their entirety on a moral code to work in a legal code country in the first place.

IN BRUNEI, WORK ADHERES TO A DIFFERENT SENSE OF TIME

Another reason for Japanese failures abroad is to be found in the similarities that exist between the Moral Code and Religious Code, despite the drastically different value systems underlying them. These similarities can generate misunderstandings.

For example, warm hospitality, the unwritten principle of reciprocity, and respect for elders are common to both regions. The practices of introducing trusted acquaintances to people who might be helpful to them, and of building long-term relationships of trust through exchanges of favors are fundamentally the same. However, displays of generous hospitality do not necessarily indicate that you are being trusted or have been accepted into the group. This is because, ultimately, the inhabitants of the Religious Code region do not fully trust those whom they regard as infidel. Also, insofar as perceptions of time are concerned, Muslims believe that "the future is in God's hands," and therefore feel less bound by future commitments. The tendency among many Muslims not to place great value on honoring time commitments can occasionally give rise to problems.

An acquaintance of mine told me of his experience building a home for a Muslim client. Although the design kept changing during the building process, pushing construction costs up, the client had no intention of paying for these modifications, much to my acquaintance' s chagrin. This particular case shows how business behavior can be predicated upon a cultural sense of time.

I myself have encountered this sense of time that followers of Islam appear to share. It occurred when I was invited to the Islamic nation of Brunei by a company under the direct control of the national government. Although I had been told that my hosts would take care of the flight arrangements, the days passed without a word from them. I finally received my flight number and times two days prior to departure. Still, there was no information about who would meet me at the airport or at what time. I was stupefied to realize that business interactions in Brunei were governed by a different temporality. Of course, as I came to learn, sometimes all we need to do is stand in faith and wait for the time when everything will fall into its perfect place.

Because these societies are male-dominated, women often find themselves trapped by an invisible wall. This feature is more conspicuous in the Middle East, and relatively less pronounced in ASEAN Islamic countries. Anyone who is serious about doing business in these societies, however, must begin with a firm understanding of the mainstream principles, rather than being confounded by exceptions.

GUIDED BY THE GLOBAL NAVIGATOR

Let's look now at the Global Navigator, the central component of the Cultural World Map (page 118). The Global Navigator organizes information along the axes of space and time with the aim to provide insight into the mental make-up of the inhabitants of each region. As can be seen, the cultural tides that have risen and fallen from ancient times (below) to the present (above) are represented as *historical cultural layers* along the axis of time. Traumatic incidents, such as wars or colonial occupations, are marked with dotted lines. The Navigator is meant to provide an overall picture of historical trends, while facilitating an understanding of current values in each country.

This knowledge is very important when doing business overseas. A Toyota campaign in China can serve as an illustrative example of cross-cultural advertising blunders that can occur when such knowledge is lacking. Toyota created a print ad featuring two stone lions bowing in front of a Toyota automobile, which prompted scathing criticism from the Chinese side. The stone lion is considered a symbol of Chinese authority, and the image of China bowing down before Japan brought back traumatic memories of Japan's invasion of China. Many pointed out that the incident occurred because Toyota's young employees in Japan were unaware of this historical trauma.

The Global Navigator is of course helpful in developing familiarity with local partners, understanding clients, and doing managerial work in foreign countries. It also offers the additional benefit of preventing the Japanese from expecting the impossible.

CHAPTER 6 A BIRD'S EYE VIEW: THE CULTURAL WORLD MAP (THE SECOND PATH)

⟨Global Navigator⟩

1) Time axis: the substance of tradition
(sample of "Cultural Layers of Tradition")

Germany: Cultural Layers of Tradition
(see Global Navigator for full version)

Germany : "Cultural Layers of Tradition"

Division & Reunification
- Fall of Berlin Wall & Reunification of Germany(1989)
- Founding Member of European Union
- Cold War & Division of East & West Germany

· Cold War &
· Soviet Influence

Nationalism & Imperialism
· WWII
- Rise of Third Reich & Defeat of Germany in World War II (1945)
- World War I (1914-1918) & Waimar Republic (1919-1933)
· WWI
- Unification of Germany States & German Empire(1871)

Protestant Reformation
- Napoleonic Invasion marks end of Holy Roman Empire(1806)
- Thirty Years War(1618) & Peace of Westphalia(1648) leave Germany weakened & disunited

· Napoleonic Invasion
- Division between Catholic and Protestant German states, sparked by Martin Luther's dissent against abuse of power by Roman Catholic Church (1517)

For instance, Japanese companies have built a reputation as world leaders in manufacturing. This accomplishment derives from a tradition of remarkable commitment to quality, which in its turn can be traced back to Shintoist beliefs that spiritual force can be infused into otherwise lifeless objects, as well as to other long-standing cultural practices. However, this culturally specific commitment to quality in manufacturing can be difficult to explain to non-Japanese who are unfamiliar with these values. A more effective approach might be to start with teaching about Japanese ways of thinking and cultural traditions.

The following countries are featured in the Global Navigator:

- Asia – China (including Hong Kong), Taiwan, Japan, Korea, Thailand, Singapore, Malaysia, Vietnam, Indonesia, the Philippines, Brunei, India, Pakistan
- Oceania – Australia, New Zealand
- Europe – The United Kingdom, Germany, France, Austria, the Netherlands, Spain, Italy, Poland
- The Middle East – Saudi Arabia
- North America – The United States, Canada
- The Russian Federation – Russia
- Latin America – Mexico, Brazil, Argentina

Currently the Global Navigator covers 30 countries, with plans for future additions.

CHAPTER 6 A BIRD'S EYE VIEW: THE CULTURAL WORLD MAP (THE SECOND PATH)

〈Global Navigator (continued)〉
2) Spatial axis: Cultural Motivators and Demotivators for Germany (Sample)

"Cultural Motivators(sm)" for Germans

"Cultural Motivators(sm)"	Key Points
1. Seriousness	• Germans appreciate "matter of fact" presentations and argumentation. • Using superlatives and generally making things look better than they are is seen as being superficial. • Beginning a meeting or presentation with a joke can cost credibility.
2. Status & Prestige	• Gaining status & prestige is a strong motivator. • Outstanding professional qualifications, such a professorship, advan[ced degrees] like a Ph.D., are high[ly valued] and should be made [known].
3. Obeying the Rules & Punctuality	• Strictly obeying the r[ules and] time is important. • Germans feel socially [obliged to] point out on the spot [when someone] has transgressed a r[ule]. • Punctuality is expecte[d as an] important factor of professionalism. If yo[u are late] for an appointment, b[e sure to] call, and have a solid [reason]. If you are late for a m[eeting, the] door may be closed a[nd it may] be rather disruptive to [enter]. • Sticking to delivery sc[hedules] is absolutely essentia[l].
4. Perfection	• Germans place an ex[treme] value on – and const[antly strive] for – perfection. • Very high quality stan[dards are a] consequence of the p[erfection] value.

"Cultural deMotivators(sm)" for Germans

"Cultural deMotivators(sm)"	Key Points
1. Over Familiarity	• Most European executives and professionals prefer to communicate with each other on a last name basis. In the German language, this takes the *Hoeflichkeitsform* – which is a grammatical style equivalent to the 3rd-person plural in English • Don't make the mistake of going to a first name basis far too early in a relationship; this will somewhat ironically make your colleague uncomfortable and less willing to be candid in discussions. • When beginning and ending a meeting, it is common for all parties to shake hands. Eye contact during these interactions are extremely important, belying your grace and manners.
2. Discussion of Sensitive or Personal Topics	• Religion is considered a private affair, and WWII or national politics are not considered appropriate topics of conversation until a good friendship has been established. • If discussing things German, be absolutely sure you know what you are talking about. In casual conversation do not ask "So what do you do?" as this is too personal. • Do not discuss personal finances or private family matters. Many Germans have strong feelings and misgivings about each other (including newly joined Easterners) so best avoid personal gossip entirely. • Acceptable topics of casual conversation are sports (especially soccer), exotic travel locales, and music.

CULTURAL MOTIVATORS (SM) AND CULTURAL DEMOTIVATORS (SM)

Factors that are attuned to local values are highlighted in the Global Navigator as cultural motivators, while factors that incite opposition appear as cultural demotivators. The initial, extensive sets of factors specific to each country have been narrowed down to the top 15. In the case of China, regional features have been included in the list in order to do justice to its vast territory. Understanding these cultural motivators and cultural demotivators affords us a glimpse into the mental make-up of people inhabiting distinct cultural worlds.

Consider the following episode, which took place as a Canadian multinational was negotiating the purchase of a business in Argentina. Managers met in Canada to work out the terms of the acquisition. All that was left was to have the vice president in Argentina sign the final papers. Several months went by, however, without any news of the signature. Reminders sent to the vice president were met with nothing but excuses. The Canadian manager then referred to the motivators in the Global Navigator and realized that Argentinians prefer direct communication. He promptly handed a letter to a colleague headed to Argentina on other business, asking her to speak to the vice president in person. The colleague was invited to dinner, and, while enjoying a pleasant evening in the vice president's company, was able to have him sign the needed documents. The North American style of virtual communication had proved insufficient to ignite the Argentinian vice president's motivation.

While there are plenty of success stories like this one, there are also numerous examples of unsuccessful ventures, caused by failures to understand differences in mental make-up. One famous example is Texas Instruments' expansion in Mexico. Although Mexico shares a border with the US, its motivators are very different. For instance, Mexicans look first at the whole picture, and only then seek to understand points of detail. But Texas Instruments did not take this approach. Instead, they started with training in machinery operation, to the dissatisfaction of the Mexican workers who wanted to know why Texas Instruments had decided to build a factory in Mexico in the first place.

Like Argentinians, Mexicans believe that matters of importance are best discussed in person, while American staff handle important affairs via email - another discrepancy between what is considered proper business practice in the two countries. Failure to consider these differences had detrimental effects on quality improvement processes and resulted in serious complaints from customers.

Excerpts from the Global Navigator are included at the end of this book for reference.

Four Cultural Codes

Code	Fields toward which values converge	Region
Legal Code	Rules and know-how	USA, Canada except Quebec, England and the rest of the UK, Scandinavian countries (Sweden, Norway, Denmark, etc.)
Moral Code	Interpersonal relations	Asia (excluding Islamic countries), Latin America, in Southern Europe, Central Africa, Russia, etc.
Religious Code	Divine teachings	The Middle East (excluding Israel, a Moral-Legal Mixed Code country, and Lebanon, a Religious-Moral Mixed Code country), Kazakhstan, Pakistan, Bangladesh, Malaysia, , Brunei, North Africa
Mixed Code	A combination of at least two codes (legal, moral, and religious)	Australia, New Zealand, India, Germany, the Netherlands, Israel, Central and Southern Africa (excluding Moral Code countries)

World Business Rules (summary)

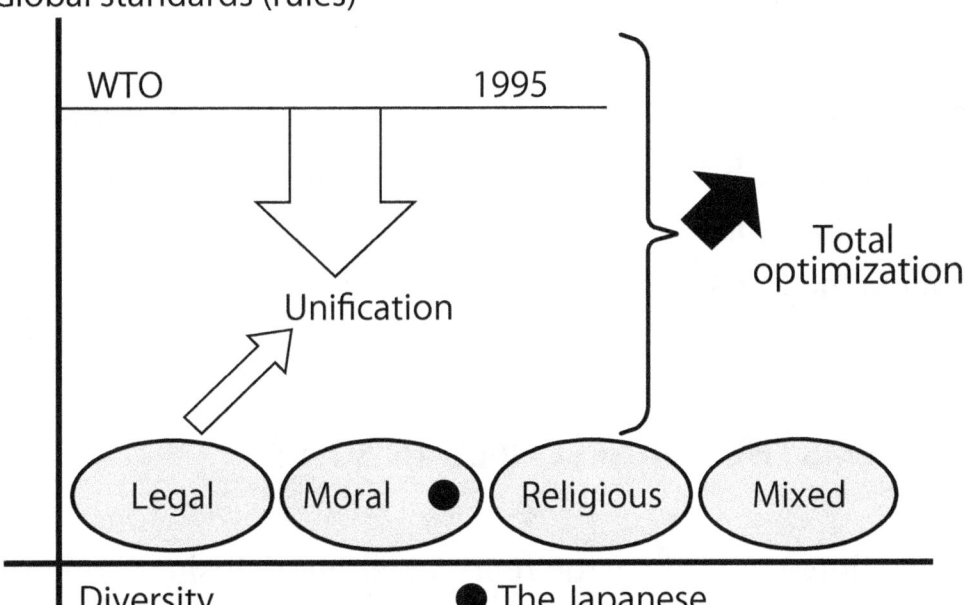

① Legal and Moral Codes rest on opposite worldviews
② Moral and Religious Code have some common values

FILLING IN THE BLANKS ON THE MENTAL MAP

As I completed the map, the world's diversity of cultures appeared to me like a fine Persian rug, in which similarities and differences were intricately woven together. I came to understand cultural diversity as a matter of how the various shades, textures and patterns are combined.

For example, the Japanese are often guilty of lumping together the cultures of Europe and the US into what they refer to as "Euro-American culture." On the flip side, they also believe that the culture of each European country must be studied individually to be properly understood. This ambivalence puts them somewhat at a loss on how to proceed.
However, when examining these countries in terms of the codes discussed above, it becomes possible to differentiate between the US and Northern European countries, which are dominated by the Legal Code, and the Moral Code countries of Southern Europe.

Of course, there will be exceptions. There will likely be times when you are unsure how to classify a particular country. Our first priority, however, is to fill in the blanks of our mental map. This is done by dividing the world up according to the four codes with the aim to lay down a global-scale foundation.

THREE PROBLEMS THE JAPANESE NEED TO SOLVE

The following figure is a schematic representation of business rules in the global era, shown along the two axes of regulations and diversity that we have discussed. Let me reiterate that the essence of global management is about pursuing total optimization based on the mental bird's eye view of the world that these two axes afford.

If we analyze the hundreds of mistakes that Japanese companies and their staff have made over the past two decades of globalization, we can classify their causes as follows.

Problem A: Insufficient attention to unified rules when doing business in the global market.
Problem B: Failure to act as ethical global citizens when conducting business in non-sovereign countries.
Problem C: Lack of knowledge regarding core aspects of the value systems associated with each cultural code.

Top managers of Japanese corporations often draw on global HR training programs at GE, IBM, and Samsung as a model for what they believe to be the latest in HR training: sending new staff overseas within two years of hiring, or conducting overseas language training. Before adopting such measures, however, management needs to resolve the three problems just mentioned. Let us now consider each one of them in detail.

1) Compliance with unified rules

The importance of unified rules (Problem A) can be difficult to appreciate for Moral Code countries like Japan. During the period when the "international model" was prevalent, many businesses adopted a "when in Rome do as the Romans do" attitude. Bribery was rampant, with large sums of money being paid to those in positions of authority to win contracts in developing countries. In the global era, however, such approaches are no longer regarded as a normal part of doing business.

One indication that things were no longer the same came fifteen years ago, when AT&T dismissed three executives at AT&T China, including the office's Chinese president, over bribery violations. This incident occurred at a time when bribery was considered commonplace in China, and greatly shocked Western corporations as well. It became vividly clear that times had changed.

Nevertheless, Japanese corporations still struggle with understanding these changes. They instead run into conflicts with regulations providing severe penalties for businesses that interfere with fair competition. In news reported by newspapers in 2012 alone, Japanese corporations paid a total of roughly 220 billion Japanese yen in fines in the US, Japan, and the EU. This does not include the 94 billion yen Toyota paid to settle the class action lawsuit seeking recovery for economic losses from the recall of Toyota automobiles in the US. According to an article in the Nikkei Shimbun of May 8, 2013, Japanese companies had been involved in half of the US antitrust cases exposed from 2011 to 2012, having paid fines which accounted for 40 percent of the total amount - the largest set of fines imposed on an individual country. During my time in the US, I felt that Japan in particular tended to disregard rules.

In order to eliminate this problem, it is important to become fully familiar with the competition laws of the US, Japan, the EU, and other target countries. It is also necessary to compile a collection of case studies analyzing the mistakes that Japanese companies have made abroad over the past two decades. In addition, the company president (not the PR manager) needs to frequently convey, to both staff and the public, the company's commitment to abide by the rules of fair competition wherever in the world they happen to do business. Justifications such as the following should never be used:

"Other corporations are also doing it. We are just accidental victims."

"The US is also strapped financially, so they are making sanctions more stringent."

"Although the conditions were unacceptable, we went ahead with the reconciliation to avoid adverse impacts on our core business."

"What a relief it didn't happen at our Japanese headquarters!"

These types of statements not only are of little benefit to all concerned, but also amount to admitting that you are not a global professional.

2) Acting as an ethical global citizen

Problem B, as formulated above, consists of the failure to act as an ethical global citizen when conducting business with non-sovereign countries. It is important to respect the laws, values, and lifestyles of the people living in the countries where you do business. This means not behaving with condescension toward local staff, and avoiding the assumption that they should be grateful for having a job. It means not displaying an attitude of superiority, as well as learning about and showing concern for past tragic events that citizens in that country might still struggle with. It means using common sense as a global citizen when going abroad. Especially in countries where memories of Japanese imperialism still resonate strongly, educating yourself on history is a crucial task before visiting. There are some who believe that the Japanese have been unfairly blamed for past acts. While I respect their opinions, I also want to emphasize the importance of understanding traumatic histories in order to work as a global citizen in a particular country.

3) Understanding the value systems informing each culture
Problem C is the lack of knowledge regarding core aspects of the value systems associated with each cultural code. To gain such knowledge it is of course necessary to consult the literature and other sources that are central to the cultural codes operating in each country. For example, learning about democratic principles is the quickest way to understand Legal Code countries. One should become familiar with the US Declaration of Independence, Constitution, Bill of Rights, and competition law (in other words, with the legislation concerning basic human rights, equal opportunity, fair competition, etc.). While it may seem unnecessary for Japanese people to learn anew about the Moral Code, in reality many Japanese lack a clear understanding of Eastern modes of thinking. Additionally, given that the Moral Code region includes numerous Catholic countries, knowledge of the Old Testament is crucial. And also, in order to better understand the Religious Code of Islam it is necessary to learn about the precepts expressed in the Quran.

As some readers may have realized, this is the type of subject matter commonly taught in liberal arts programs. And they couldn't be more right. In order to compete in the global market, it is important to ground oneself in universally shared values, which spring from traditions such as those of the world religions and Eastern thought.

Of course, in each region there are other religions and ideologies that exist intermingled with one another. Not everyone on the planet believes in a world religion, nor are all the inhabitants of Asia equally influenced by Eastern philosophy. What matters most, given these conditions, is the capacity of the mind, its power to receive and hold ideas and knowledge. Be concerned first with developing a maximum capacity for understanding, then gradually create mental drawers that you pack tightly with knowledge and wisdom. This is the learning method that will prepare you for the challenges of our new age.

In Japanese universities, students rarely study the liberal arts. Or rather, because they do not learn about the liberal arts in a systematic fashion, they end up with mere "knowledge." The Cultural World Map can serve as a helpful framework when studying the liberal arts. This is why several major corporations which emphasize these kinds of values in their organization have adopted the Cultural World Map as a learning tool.

SCRAPBOOKING

One of the quickest ways to cultivate a bird's eye view of the world is by scrapbooking. First, start off reading paper versions of newspapers. As you cut and paste bits of information you will increase your intelligence about the world around you. While there is no one correct way of scrapbooking, I would like to share the method I have been using.

I began by preparing nine scrapbooks - one for each of the seven world regions, and two separate ones for Russia, and Japan. In time, this categorization proved unsatisfactory, so, as needed, I went on to classify scrapbooks by country, topic, and client. For those just starting out, however, a region-based categorization would certainly help steer them on the right path. Newspapers are the most important source of material for scrapbooks, (I subscribe to two newspapers focusing on opinion and the economy). However, related quality articles from weekly magazines and foreign English-language media can also be added. In a first stage, you take a broad view, selecting events that strike you as important in the history of humankind. The second stage can be more customized to individual needs, so feel free to cut and paste prominent news relating to your field of interest. Care should be taken not to be overzealous in cutting out articles and amassing more information than one can practically handle. Also, one should not aim for the elegance of a masterpiece. My scrapbooks, full as they are of underlined passages and circled words, are definitely not designed to impress others! Because scrapbooks are not carefully organized compositions, it is important not to use them in isolation, but rather in conjunction with other related material. The purpose in scrapbooking is to understand the step-by-step evolution of your mental map of the world. A scrapbook of disheveled newspaper clippings works great for that purpose. As you reread your scrapbooks, you realize that you have somehow overlooked important news, and make other discoveries as well. Scrapbooking will make it easier to grasp how recent events fit into large-scale axes of time and space. It is definitely worth giving a try.

CHAPTER 7
ETHICS AND THE LEGAL MIND (THE THIRD PATH)

THE JAPANESE AND THE MORAL CODE

As our discussion so far has shown, the Japanese fit perfectly the profile of a society dominated by a moral code. In Japan, interpersonal relationships are a driving force of business, the ability to work well with others is vital, and a ubiquitous motto states that the "customer should be treated like a god." After returning to Japan, the first advice I received was to attach an honorific suffix to company names, and to write those names at the top of the page when drafting proposals for clients.

Such practices are not necessarily bad. Japanese culture has special traditions according to which spirits are believed to dwell in inanimate objects, and memorial services are held to honor sewing needles and stuffed animals that have reached the end of their useful lives. The belief that an object can be imbued with spirit has nurtured a culture of excellence in manufacturing and craftsmanship. That is an amazing accomplishment.

However, to make further progress, the Japanese need to become aware of the fact that they belong to the Moral Code cultural region. Failure to realize this will cause them to run, again and again, into significant misunderstandings. So how can the Japanese avoid such misunderstandings and achieve world-class competitiveness? A quick solution is to master two forms of soft power: ethics and the legal mind, which are but two sides of the same coin.

ETHICS VERSUS MORALITY

When I mention "ethics," I am sometimes asked how they differ from morality. Not so long ago, I spoke at a research seminar about the introduction of moral education into Japanese schools, a topic that has generated a great deal of controversy. I pointed out that, from a global perspective, both ethics *and* morality should be taught to young students. My opinion was severely criticized by the seasoned education veterans and moral education experts attending the seminar, who insisted that morality and ethics were one and the same thing. In America, or at least on the East Coast, which had been my base of operations for twenty-five years, it was common sense to distinguish between ethics and morality. I found it hard to believe that in Japan the terms were considered synonymous. As I scanned the editorial and opinion pages of a number of newspapers, I was relieved to find that these two concepts were actually differentiated in Japan as well. Unfortunately, certain education specialists fail to draw this distinction and erroneously lump the two terms together.

Ethics are universal principles that transcend time and setting, defining appropriate behavior for all human beings. Morality, on the other hand, consists of standards prescribing what is considered virtuous in a specific period or environment.

An example that is easy to understand is slavery. During the time when slavery was still alive and thriving, one white man reportedly boasted, "I am very kind to my slaves. I take them with me to church every Sunday, and provide them supper. I consider myself morally upright." This man may have been morally upright by the standards of his time. But he failed to realize that the act of owning slaves was unethical in and of itself.

The country's long history of slavery aside, the US shares with the rest of the Legal Code region a tendency to draw a clear distinction between ethics and morality. The importance of a solid understanding of ethics becomes clear once we pause to consider the tremendous influence that Legal Code countries have had on the creation of unified rules and international standards in the global age, their high rankings in terms of global competiveness, and the expectation that global leaders be well versed in the Legal Code.

In today's world, there are countries who seek to impose their own logic on others in ways incompatible with shared global values. Such countries rely on coercion by expanding their military might, believe themselves entitled to use any means in pursuit of national interest, base their actions on the principle of retaliation, and dominate other ethnic groups by force. Attempts to invoke morality to denounce such acts will be of limited effect. The only way to combat these oppressive powers is to rely on ethics, whose principles transcend the particularities of time and space, defining what constitutes proper conduct for the human being, and on an ethically grounded Legal Code.

A LACK OF LEGAL AWARENESS

The second soft power we will discuss here, the cultivation of a "legal mind," has also proved challenging to the Japanese, as they struggle to understand its subtleties. In 1982, six people from Hitachi and Mitsubishi Electronics were arrested on grounds of industrial espionage involving the theft of confidential information from IBM headquarters in the US. But at that time the Japanese media paid little attention to the importance of respecting intellectual property rights. Instead, they focused their energies on collectively condemning the sting operation that the FBI conducted to prove that there was spying going on.

In 1996, the US Equal Employment Opportunity Commission filed a class action lawsuit against Mitsubishi Motor Manufacturing of America, claiming that the company had failed to put an end to sexual harassment and gender discrimination against its female employees. According to the company's statements reported in the media, Mitsubishi did not recognize sexual harassment as a violation of basic human rights, but rather dismissed it as merely vulgar, insisting that it was American employees who were at fault, and that the Japanese staff had nothing to do with it.

Then there was the Olympus scandal. In 2011, British-born Michael Woodford, the CEO of Japanese camera maker Olympus, conducted an internal investigation that uncovered financial irregularities related to corporate acquisitions. Following the investigation, he urged the company's chairman and vice president to take responsibility for these schemes by resigning. The response of the Olympus board of directors was an application of the Moral Code: they found Woodford guilty of arbitrary management and dismissed him as unfit for the role of CEO. Later, however, the investigation that Woodford started led to the arrest and trial of senior Olympus executives, who thus ended up being judged according to the Legal Code.

This series of incidents shows that over the past thirty years, the Japanese have been slow in developing a legal mind. The rest of the world, in the meantime, has entered the age of globalization, and it is now a matter of general consensus that actions running counter to free competition will be penalized according to the Legal Code.

Of course, I am not trying to propose an essentialist view of the Japanese as innately lacking any form of legal mind. Rather, I wish to point to a problem of education. In cultural regions under the strong monotheistic influence of Judaism, Christianity, and Islam, religious ethics have provided a solid bedrock for ethical education. This does not mean that the prescriptions of the legal code are followed to the letter. After all, it is these regions that have been the greatest violators of the fundamental ethical principle, "thou shall not kill."

On the other hand, the fact that in Japan lost items are often returned to the owner is considered by many a sign of the upstanding moral character of the Japanese. While this is still different from having a sense of ethics, it is not entirely far-fetched to believe that, with the right balance of morality, ethics and a legal mind, Japan could become a significant player in creating a new world order.

RECOGNIZING THE RULE OF LAW AS ABSOLUTE

How is it possible to become versed in ethical and legal ways of thinking? To develop these skills, the Japanese will need a keener awareness of the things they currently cannot do in the international arena. They also have much to learn from the negative examples set by certain neighboring countries.

First, Japan would benefit from a renewed recognition of the absolute character of the rule of law. There is an urgent need for Japan not only to understand what the shared rules for global business are, but also to play a more active role in their creation.

The "rule of law" should also serve as the foundation for Japan's responses to unreasonable pressures from neighboring countries. Sovereignty issues over the Senkaku Islands, for example, have caused Japan's relations with China to deteriorate, triggering a host of economic problems. Nevertheless, Japan has been unable to address this incident in a clear-cut manner. As it pursues the resolution of these issues, Japan should consistently rely on the rule of law.

For instance, before the publication in the New York Times of advertisements stating that the Senkaku Islands were Chinese territory, Japan should have used major international newspapers to clarify the legal bases for its sovereignty claims over the islands. Japan should also make public a list of corrections to the errors and fabrications that China has released officially. The biggest problem is letting these kinds of statements go unchecked.

As a participant at the World Expo 2005 in Japan's Aichi Prefecture, I organized an exhibit of textbooks from several major countries with the intention to showcase how they described Japan and the Japanese. German textbooks were the most accurate, while Vietnamese ones were the most fraught with errors. To my surprise, almost all of the textbooks contained unabashed misinformation. One should not therefore assume that facts are faithfully and diligently communicated across the world. Rather, it is our responsibility to be proactive in ensuring that correct information is made available.

THE LOCALS ARE ATTENTIVE OBSERVERS

It is also necessary to have a basic stance of respect for local cultural codes, with their rules, values and lifestyles, and to interact with all people in a spirit of equality and fairness.

Today, fewer employers are inclined to look down upon local people as uncivilized, to act arrogantly as if they are doing them a favor by hiring them, or to discriminate women in the workplace. However, it is still commonplace for the voices of local staff to be stifled.

But local people in the areas where we do business are observing us carefully. Here is how someone in a Southeast Asian country describes relationships between a certain Japanese supervisor and his locally hired employees: the supervisor considered locals ignorant, and made a habit of harshly reprimanding them in front of others when they made a mistake. To the local staff, however, it was precisely this kind of behavior that appeared as pitifully uncivilized. In addition to ethics education, therefore, it is important to learn about the leadership requirements specific to each cultural region. What type of leaders will local people respect and follow?

UNDERSTANDING THE WORLD'S PERSPECTIVES ON INTERNATIONAL INCIDENTS

The Japanese are out of their element when it comes to dual-axis thinking. For example, whenever a Japanese national becomes involved in an act of terror, the Japanese side tends to emphasize respect for human life as the foremost value. In contrast, the judgments underlying the actions of the international community are based on a dual-axis matrix, which gives equal priority to terrorism deterrence (hunting down all the perpetrators of terror, and avoiding the payment of ransom). The Japanese have a hard time understanding this reasoning, and run into disputes with foreigners over international issues concerning Japan.

For example, the Japanese have been criticized for their tendency to see themselves exclusively as victims of the atomic bomb attacks on Hiroshima and Nagasaki, while forgetting that it was Japan that started the war in the Pacific. Such criticism is bound to raise objections in Japan, yet it is nonetheless important to understand that this is the international point of view.

It has been nearly five years since, one evening, I attended a business reception at a riverside location in Singapore, together with guests from other Asian countries. I do not remember how the topic came up, but, as the liquor started to take effect, the Asian participants whom I thought I was on friendly terms with started criticizing Japan for doing business in countries they had invaded during World War II without having ever apologized. Although I replied that Japan had already expressed its apologies, no one would listen. The argument escalated to the point where I feared for my physical safety. Later, as I reflected on this incident, I came to realize the importance of being well acquainted with ethics and the legal code.

PROBLEMS ARISING FROM AN ABSENCE OF LEGAL AWARENESS

Understanding what is and is not correct is essential in the formation of a legal mind.
Although nowadays there is much indignation among the Japanese over Chinese imitation products and patent infringement, Japan tended to overlook the importance of intellectual property rights up until the IBM industrial espionage incident of 1982. Information was considered free, and bringing along some desired piece of information to share was common practice when calling on one's business partners. For Americans inhabiting a Legal Code society, this Japanese practice must have appeared culturally backward. The Japanese today have a considerably higher level of legal awareness than they did in those days. And yet, having returned to Japan

after doing business for 25 years in a Legal Code society, I still find it insufficient.

Here are some examples of problems stemming directly from the lack of legal awareness of the Japanese:

- A number of major Japanese corporations still do not sign non-disclosure agreements or business contracts when requesting work.
- Some Japanese participants in my seminars have replaced the original cover of the seminar notes with one bearing their own name or the name and logo of their company (apparently with no qualms whatsoever).
- Whenever a problem occurs, I tend to exclude considerations of relationships, character or personality in order to identify the real underlying causes of the problem and work toward their elimination. This, however, has brought me criticism that I was speaking badly about others.
- It is still common practice to copy expensive software because "others are doing it."
- Quotes from books and other people's ideas are often used without proper acknowledgment of the source.
- While I do not reject the Japanese practice of sending mid and year-end gifts, there is no awareness in Japan that offering expensive gifts to prospective clients, or wining and dining them at high-end restaurants can be perceived as corruption or preferential treatment.
- Interpersonal relationships are often brought into contract negotiations.
- Even after signing a contract, parties may show little awareness of having made a commitment. This often results in broken promises.
- As the Olympus scandal showed, there are cases in which inconvenient truths are hidden, smothered up, or kept silent to prevent

them from coming to light. Those who fail to do so are criticized as uncaring.

What all these problems have in common is a tendency to leave the underlying causes of problems unexamined, to evade accountability for one's actions, and to assume that all people are fundamentally the same. This attitude is characteristic of a Moral Code society.

In the US, a crime is considered more serious when one attempts to hide evidence or engage in behind-the-scenes maneuvering. Businesses that dodge accountability can end up being dragged into court by shareholders. Of course, Legal Code societies have their own major scandals triggered by unethical conduct. But still, these societies are characterized by the presence of powerful deterrent forces. The Olympus scandal illustrates this point clearly: the British-born president was determined to carry out his investigation into the company's misconduct at the risk of losing his job, which testifies to his high level of legal awareness.

LEARNING FROM OTHERS' MISTAKES

Territorial disputes often cause a great flutter in Japan. Witnessing these reactions, I cannot but admit that Japan still has a long way to go before it learns how to deal with these issues. The main problem is that, in addressing international controversies, the Japanese rely once again on the Moral Code.

For starters, when a country's spokesperson states that "the Japanese stole the Senkaku Islands," and describes reports of fire control radars having been directed at Japanese navy vessels as complete fabrications, or otherwise as Japan's attempts to incite a crisis and disgrace China, such behavior only lacks in common sense; it verges on madness. Appeals to morality become irrelevant when faced with such a dialogue partner. Because resorting to lies to deny another nation's legitimate claims is a violation of ethics in the first place. This is why, in order to respond effectively to such rash acts and prevent being overpowered by neighboring countries in the long term, it is crucial to

1) Rely on the rule of law.
2) Support your case with facts.
3) Ground your ethnic identity in a strong sense of ethics.
4) Bring the legitimacy of your cause to the attention of international opinion.

In other words, what is needed is a shift in emphasis from the Moral Code, with its preoccupation for morality, high context (communication reliant on interpersonal relationships and specific circumstances), and interactions based on regard for and consideration of others, to a legal mind that attaches importance to ethics, fact-based communication, and public relations. It is also important in dealing with such issues to use matrix thinking, including a firm grasp of the axis of time. The Japanese need to understand that one of the reasons why controversial historical issues keep resurfacing is that their perception of the temporal axis has so far failed to gain global recognition. Consequently, they should adopt one that is more properly anchored to facts.

BALANCING CULTURAL CODES

In this book, I have emphasized the importance of the Legal Code primarily because the Japanese tend to be deficient in this area. This does not mean that one should rely wholly on the Legal Code at all times. Whenever the values of one code garner enough power to dominate over the others, the risk of a negative impact on society increases. Thus,

- excessive emphasis on the Legal Code will lead to a litigious society;
- excessive emphasis on the Moral Code will lead to a bullying society;
- excessive emphasis on the Religious Code will lead to a terrorist society.

In conclusion, to qualify as global talent one needs to blend together the strengths of these various cultural codes in a balanced and thoughtful way. When I ask Japanese business professionals who have a solid understanding of these codes how they incorporate them into their work, most estimate that they rely on the Moral Code about 80-90% of the time. The Moral Code approach, however, does not carry much currency in the global market. As a more viable alternative, I propose using the 60/30/10 rule: you rely 60% on the cultural code into which you were born and within which you were raised. For someone from Japan, this means reducing the focus on the Moral Code to 60%. In addition, at least 30% of their attention should be devoted to the Legal Code. Finally, at least 10% should be allocated to the Religious Code, and its associated reverence for a higher power. While the Japanese might find the Religious Code difficult to comprehend, it is important to remember that reverence for a higher power also lies at the heart of Shintoism, which can be helpful in understanding the experience of those who believe in monotheistic religions.

In the next chapter, we will touch upon this theme of religious experience in more detail.

CHAPTER 8
REFINING JAPANESE CULTURAL DNA TO NURTURE JAPANESE-STYLE GLOBAL TALENT (THE FOURTH PATH)

JAPANESE CULTURAL DNA

Recently, there has been a significant increase in foreign hires at Japanese companies. Given the shortage of genuine global talent in Japan, this trend is only natural. At the current rate, by the time Japanese students of today join the workforce, they will likely encounter not only Americans and Europeans, but also Chinese, Koreans and Indians in the upper echelons of Japanese companies.

There are some who believe that the recruitment of foreign employees is a sign that Japanese companies are becoming globalized. However, while I consider myself one of the least discriminatory people out there, I feel alarmed by this trend. For Japan to be a top player in the international arena, businesses should instead focus on *Japanese cultural DNA* as an essential ingredient in developing global talent. Neglecting this need, while simply continuing to increase the number of foreign hires could have adverse effects.

One of the many problems with global talent education in Japan is that it ignores Japanese identity. Both the axis of shared global values and the axis of Japanese cultural DNA, as expressed in the nation's traditions, have an important role to play in the development of true global talent.

So, just what is Japanese cultural DNA?

As a field of scholarship, Japanese cultural DNA has attracted the attention of numerous academics and other experts. Here, I would like to expand on two of its constituents, which have emerged as particularly important in light of my twenty-five years of experience overseas: first, the belief in the providence of nature, and second, Shintoism.

As pointed out by Masahiko Nakanishi, head of the National Vision Society, and Masatoshi Tsuchiya in their co-authored book, *The Decline of Christian Civilization* (2007, JPS Publishing), as well as by Tatsuo Kobayashi, Professor Emeritus at Kokugakuin University, the belief in natural providence became ingrained in Japanese cultural DNA during the ten thousand years of the Jomon period. Shintoism, in its turn, stands out as uniquely Japanese when we consider the forms spirituality has taken in Japanese, Chinese and Korean cultures, all of which belong to the Confucian cultural region.

WHY DID JAPAN BECOME A MANUFACTURING POWER?

I like to think that the Japanese cultural DNA shaped Japan's transformation into a manufacturing or *monozukuri* power. During my time in the US, it was common for Japanese companies to perceive American-made products as defective and inferior in quality, which constituted a major source of friction between the two sides. US executives versed in the Japanese ways of doing business would travel in person to Japan to apologize to clients for product-related problems. But in doing so, they were simply acting out of concern that they might lose their Japanese clients.

Oftentimes, the US side would argue that, "their products conformed to global standards," that "it was not fair for Japan to receive preferential treatment," and that "allowances should be made for some degree of human and machine error."

The belief that all people should be treated equally has indeed been part of the American cultural DNA since the Declaration of Independence. It is also true that Americans tend to see manufacturing in terms of science and technology rather than craftsmanship. But this understanding actually limits the ability of the US to compete with Japan on quality standards in manufacturing. The Japanese understanding of manufacturing is informed by Shintoist ideas which hold that part of a craftsman's soul is transferred to the object he makes. Japan's outstanding skill in *monozukuri* derives from the fusion of this traditional notion of craftsmanship with the American science and philosophy of quality management (W. Edwards Deming's fourteen management principles), along with the Chinese spirit of the "Way" as a driving force of advancement and improvement, and with the Japanese management method of attention to detail known as the "lock-in strategy."

Consider the following striking example.

I was unsure how to approach the multitude of quality discrepancies that Japanese and American companies were facing. No matter how clearly explained, the message wasn't getting across. After pondering the issue for a while, I decided to explain about the Japanese cultural DNA to staff at a certain US factory. I explained how, in the eyes of the Japanese, *monozukuri* is not subsumed to the category of science. Rather, it can be likened to a mother giving birth to a child. Just like the mother wishes for a beautiful, healthy baby, for a Japanese manufacturer, the *monozukuri* process involves pouring heart and soul into the pursuit of ultimate craftsmanship. Understood as *monozukuri*, manufacturing is the art of creation.

Having explained this, I glanced around the room, and to my surprise I saw tears welling up in the eyes of my American audience. "Now I understand," remarked one person. Thank you for taking the time to explain these things to us." Others in the room nodded in agreement. What I learned from this experience is to never give up explaining differences in cultures, assuming that your audience won't get it. If you convincingly explain how ideas and attitudes are bound up with a particular cultural background, those listening will eventually understand.

At the same time, thinking about these issues helped me appreciate anew the power of the belief that a creator's soul is projected onto the object of his creation, and its far-reaching influence on Japanese culture.

FROM MONOTHEISM TO SHINTOISM

As I mentioned previously, one could argue that the world is experiencing a shift away from religion. For as long as Western-oriented perspectives predominated, monotheism held absolute value. Now, however, its limitations are starting to show.

It can be argued that the retreat of monotheism is a consequence not only of globalization, but also of humankind's ventures into space.

Astronauts who have seen the Earth from space speak of being struck with a profound sense of awe before the vast power that orders and sustains the universe. This experience is unrelated to the astronauts' particular religious affiliation. They also report a sudden recognition that all life is interconnected and fragile, and that, when all is put in perspective, the wars that we fight over some trivial doctrinal difference appear foolish and meaningless. Our newly found ability to see our home from space may, in the long run, end up liberating us from religion, until all that is left is a sense of awe at the grandeur of nature. Is this not the same awe toward the natural world found in Shinto thought? As an alternative to monotheistic religion, the sustained reverence for nature that permeates Japanese culture is part of what makes it unique and valuable.

JAPANESE TRADITIONS AND FIVE CULTURE-SPECIFIC VALUES

What should we, the Japanese, do in order to fully understand and tap into the potentials of our cultural DNA? I believe the following three steps are essential:

1) Identifying, pursuing and refining Japanese traditions and culturally specific values;
2) Taking pride in sharing them with the world;
3) Using Japanese cultural DNA to create business models that make positive contributions to the world.

Let us now consider each of these three steps in turn.

The first step is associated with five prominent values.

1) Teamwork – a behavioral pattern characteristic of agrarian societies. It is often noted that rice cultivation, a cooperative endeavor based on intensive teamwork, left its imprint on the development of Japanese cultural DNA. This type of teamwork does not produce regimented, army-style teams. Rather, it is the coordination that arises when, as one starts sweeping the floor, someone else silently brings along a bucket of water to mop, and another person begins wiping the windows. It is about complementing one another, helping out others after you have finished your own tasks, and persevering as a group until all work is completed. The spontaneity of such teamwork is at once its defining characteristic and its strength.

2) The principle of *sogiotoshi* ("stripping away")
The aspiration to strip away everything that is superfluous, and to attune one's being to the essence of the materials (*mono*) being used characterizes Japanese arts and crafts, from interior decoration to food presentation and Japanese-style painting, I often return to this aspect when I explain Japanese culture to foreigners.

Japanese homes and artifacts are the products of an aesthetic that rejects ornamentation for the sake of ornamentation, emphasizing instead functional beauty and the essence of raw materials. While similar in certain ways to Scandinavian design, Japanese design also incorporates the subtle nuances of tradition. A classic example is Toyota's application of the *sogiotoshi* principle to car making, which contributed to the company's ascent to being one of the top motor-vehicle manufacturers in the world.

Around the time of the collapse of the Cold War system, a group of MIT researchers visited eight car makers around the world to investigate their business models. The results of their research were published in the 1990 bestseller *The Machine that Changed the World*, a book that propelled into the limelight Toyota's unique approach to manufacturing excellence. While other auto manufacturers operated on a principle of addition, constantly upgrading their cars in terms of new desirable features, Toyota relied on subtraction. The *sogiotoshi* principle of stripping away excess lay at the core of Toyota's manufacturing philosophy. This principle would later be systematized into what is today known as the "lean production system." After the book was published, the logic and techniques of the lean production system continued to capture attention, contributing to Toyota's global expansion. As I see it, Toyota's success demonstrated the potential inherent in Japanese culture more generally. Japan's strength and resourcefulness lie precisely in principles like *sogiotoshi* and its careful elimination of excess – principles that could be applied to create Japanese-style business models. Interestingly, this potential gained visibility through the work of foreign researchers. The Japanese had been unaware of their own originality.

3) "Momentary brilliance" (*setsuna no kagayaki)*, the "pathos of things" (*mono no aware*), "mysterious depth" (*yugen)*, and the "appreciation of austere beauty" (*wabi sabi))*

An array of aesthetic concepts has been associated with Japanese art and poetry: "momentary brilliance" (*setsuna no kagayaki)*, the "pathos of things," (*mono no aware*), "mysterious depth" (*yugen)*, and "the appreciation of austere beauty" (*wabi sabi)*. These terms may give expression to specifically Japanese perceptions of the world, yet the charm they hold for the international public is unmistakable.

In a world marked by intensive urbanization and the advance of IT technologies, these Japanese categories and their insights into beauty can constitute a source of powerful symbols of respite and humanity. It is no easy task, however, to fully define these terms so as to make their meanings accessible to a non-Japanese audience. Indeed, finding effective ways to explain these concepts has so far been a monumental struggle for the Japanese. How to best take advantage of Japan's aesthetic traditions is an important question that remains to be addressed.

4) The Japanese assimilation and adaptation of Eastern philosophy (particularly of the idea of *michi*, "the way")

As numerous scholars have noted, Confucianist and Buddhist thought were highly influential in the formation of Japanese cultural DNA. I would argue, however, that among the various belief systems developed in China, it was the Taoist idea of "the way" (*tao* in Chinese; *dô* or *michi* in Japanese) that had a decisive impact. *Tao* was originally understood as the principle underlying the whole of creation. In many ways, the spirit of *tao* bears similarities to the notion of a global world. Of the differences that set them apart, perhaps the most fundamental one concerns the way of life to be sought after. A life guided by the spirit of *tao* is fulfilled when consciousness awakens to the laws of nature and the universe, becoming aligned with them. On the other hand, the way of life valued in a global world is one in which power accrues to the individual as he or she goes through a process of globalization. This power can then be used to address world-scale problems and effect change.

The Japanese simplified the profound philosophy of *tao*, using the concept to refer to the energy that drives continuous self-improvement through the cultivation of spirit and skill. *Tao* was thus reinterpreted as the driving force of perseverance. It was this driving force that enabled Japan to rise from the ruins of World War II and become a leading *monozukuri* nation.

In Japan, monetary incentives are less important than the employees' commitment to bringing their product a little closer to perfection, and to performing tomorrow better than they did today. This is known as the "spirit of *michi*," an attitude that is rarely found outside Japan. On the contrary, when I visit the manufacturing sites or offices of foreign companies, I often meet tired employees, frustrated with the daily grind, who never miss an opportunity to goof off when the boss isn't looking. I often wonder what training would be necessary to instill the Japanese work ethic in foreign employees. If the value created in Japanese society by the spirit of *michi* could be translated into monetary terms, the figures would be astronomical.

5) The spirit of altruism (the desire to contribute to society)
During my work over the years with people from more than thirty different countries, I have not encountered the Japanese dedication to serving society paralleled anywhere else. Much praise has been given to the Japanese people in the aftermath of the earthquake and tsunami that struck eastern Japan in 2011, for their calm and orderliness in coping with the disaster and in organizing to care for their neighbors. This spirit of altruism is one of the distinguishing characteristics and great strengths of the Japanese. It stands out even more when considering, for instance, China's approach to development assistance in recent years. Chinese assistance programs are conditioned on heavy involvement of Chinese companies. In the long run, these programs benefit Chinese companies, focusing little on the transfer of much-needed knowledge or skills to recipient countries. In contrast, Japan's development assistance is based on technical cooperation and other strategies intended to support the recipient country's growth. It comes as no

surprise, therefore, that criticism of Chinese aid is mounting from various African countries, Iraq, Afghanistan, Myanmar, and Vietnam, while approval for Japanese-style assistance is on the rise.

Incidentally, the Japanese penchant for altruism might also be changing scientific thinking. African-born British biologist Richard Dawkins interpreted the behavior of DNA to be evolutionarily selfish in nature. In response, Japanese molecular biologist Kazuo Murakami proposed that DNA has altruistic elements. This altruistic spirit has yet to expand to permeate global perspectives in their totality. New business models referred to as "social business" which target the poorest groups at the base of the world's socio-economic pyramid, are rapidly spreading worldwide. But the models have not originated from Japan, and much terrain remains to be covered to take full advantage of their potential. The time is clearly ripe with opportunities to putting into practice the spirit of *michi*.

In this section, we have examined five values that are particularly important to the Japanese. Understanding these values and self-consciously cultivating them is the first step that I wish to highlight here.

PRESENTING THREE IDENTITIES TO THE WORLD

Let us now look in more depth at the second step, which we have described as "taking pride in sharing Japan's cultural traditions and values with the world." Up to now, the Japanese have been cautious about standing out too much while overseas, fearing that assertive behavior might create friction with the locals. They have therefore hesitated to stress the specificity of Japanese corporations, attempting instead to blend in with the local organizational culture. However, such attitudes are becoming increasingly anachronistic in the contemporary global age. To compete in the globalized world, the Japanese will need to make their collective identity more visible.

But what is this Japanese identity that the Japanese are supposed to give expression to? In my view, it encompasses the following three distinctive elements.

1) The "customer-is-God" mentality

For Japanese businesses, the customer is supreme. Of all the countries in the world, only Japan and Switzerland view the customer in this way (that being said, Swiss banks have come under significant pressure in recent years, with the result that the privacy of bank clients became difficult to protect). This idea of customer supremacy is gaining traction worldwide. For example, when Louis V. Gerstner was appointed chairman and CEO of the multinational IBM in the 1990s, the company was in desperate straits. To revive the ailing corporate giant, Gerstner reorganized all business, shifting the focus from computer technology to the customer. It was this customer-centered perspective that transformed IBM into a top-class global corporation. In this evolving context, the Japanese notion that "the customer is God" can serve as a powerful asset.

2) *Wa* management

In the early seventh century, Prince Shotoku promulgated a set of government guidelines known as the Seventeen-Article Constitution. The first article famously states the importance of the principle of *wa*, a word that can be translated into English as "harmony" or "peace." *Wa* refers to a code of conduct prescribing that those from both upper and lower classes should handle disagreements based on human morality, striving for conciliation, and thus avoiding conflicts and fights. This ideal of harmony lies at the heart of the Moral Code. The world today is plagued with riots, strikes, and countries quarrelling with one another. There is much to be appreciated about the spirit of *wa* in our current world, especially if it is disseminated in a form customized to fit current needs.

3) The knowledge-creating company

Whereas Euro-American businesses buy and sell expertise to rapidly move operations forward, Japanese companies use a "fermentation" approach to knowledge creation, allowing longer periods for the development of their own unique know-how. I used to draw on this fermentation metaphor quite often when explaining the particularities of Japanese companies to non-Japanese. Later, I read an article by Ikujiro Nonaka in the *Harvard Business Review*, titled *The Knowledge Creating Company: How Japanese Companies Create the Dynamics of Innovation*, and then the Japanese translation of his English book with the same title (Toyo Keizai Inc., 1995). Nonaka's article and book explore the interaction between tacit and explicit knowledge, and their role in systematic processes of knowledge creation in Japanese organizations. I was pleasantly surprised to find some of the ideas I had talked about developed into full-fledged theories.

Efforts to communicate the distinctively Japanese patterns of knowledge creation in terms that are simple and concise could go a long way towards promoting an accurate understanding of Japanese businesses. The ways in which these businesses operate will likely resonate with many people. This will not only place them at an advantage, but will also aid in attracting local staff who are genuinely interested and invested in these types of values, and thus easier to motivate.

THE TRUE MEANING OF SINCERITY

When I introduced the Cultural World Map earlier in this book, I pointed out that the two worlds of the Legal and the Moral Codes are inverted relative to each other, governed by diametrically opposed sets of values. The implication of this difference is that the use of literal translation to Japanese values to a Legal Code audience may generate a negative impression. Let me give an example. The Japanese word *seijitsu* is usually translated as equivalent to the English word "sincerity." In the past, interpretations of this word have led to problems in Japanese-US relations. In the 1980s, when trade frictions between Japan and the US were beginning to escalate, the Japanese side insisted that they were responding to these issues in a "sincere" manner. The nuance that the word carries in Japanese, however, denotes an attitude that is not self-serving, indicating that good faith efforts are being made. In contrast, the English word "sincerity" designates "consistency between speech and action." From a US perspective, sincerity would have meant committing to concrete figures and taking immediate action. The gulf that these misunderstandings created between the two sides proved difficult to bridge.

What can be done to prevent such misunderstandings? Rather than resorting to literal translations, it is important to use examples that capture the essence of the original. Take for instance the Japanese concepts of *honne* (true inner feelings) and *tatemae* (the social self one shows the world). When these terms are explained in English for a Legal Code audience, they are often taken to reflect a double standard. This in turn may have the unwanted effect of making the Japanese appear as a people who rely on outdated forms of communication, and undermining the credibility.

To prevent this, I have found it helpful to use an analogy between the *honne-tatemae* distinction and the complementary relationship between the reality of the theater stage and the reality of the dressing room. While *tatemae* corresponds to the performance on stage, *honne* is the dressing room behind the curtain. Everyone in the audience is aware of the existence of a backstage realm. Nonetheless, they enjoy the world unfolding on the stage before them. Similarly, *honne* and *tatemae* are equally real for the Japanese, who can simultaneously appreciate the outward expressions of the social self, and be sensitive to the inner feelings of others. Depending on the situation, they might attend to the voice of *honne* first, and later aim for consensus based on *tatemae*. This traveling back and forth between *honne* and *tatemae* makes it possible to minimize opposition and friction in relationships. It also helps in understanding people's true intentions. This is how I describe these concepts.

Here is another example. I mentioned before that, in the past, Japan used to be criticized for its inadequate protection of intellectual property rights and for its tendency to imitate foreign technologies and product designs. Every time I heard such criticism, I replied by drawing attention to the venerable Japanese tradition of seeing in nature a great teacher, and in the replication of nature the only legitimate way of learning. In this tradition, imitation was not understood as the violation of somebody else's intellectual property. Rather, it revolved on an acknowledgment of the fascination that the object of replication exerted over the mind. It sprang from a desire to become one with the object, to allow oneself to be possessed by its mystery at the end of what was, first and foremost, an exercise in self-discipline. While this is no justification for ignoring intellectual property rights, this cultural reference was effective in explaining why the idea of intellectual property presented a problem for the Japanese.

TACIT COMMUNICATION DOES NOT WORK

It is not my intention to argue against the Japanese method of "tacit communication" here. Nevertheless, I wish to draw attention to one of its major drawbacks: it is very time consuming. I recall an episode that took place in the 1990s at American Honda, a former client of mine. An employee who had been transferred from the company's Japanese headquarters told US engineering staff that they would benefit from familiarizing themselves with the "Honda Way." When the staff members asked for a written clarification of what the Honda Way was, their Japanese colleague gave the following answer: "The moment you try to explain the Honda Way in writing, the meaning is lost. It can only be learned in the actual experience of daily work." As I later sought to understand what exactly the Honda Way was, I found an intricate assemblage of Western and Japanese values, which defied literal translation. It was also clear, however, that learning the Honda Way on the job would require an incredible amount of time.

It appears though that times have changed. Recently, I had a conversation with someone who had worked with Carlos Ghosn on the reforms at Nissan, producing the documents that gave textual expression to the Nissan Way. For this translation project, the person had to find the right words with which to describe the spirit of this Japanese corporation for a non-Japanese audience. It had been a success story, and, listening about it, I realized that the Japanese had become more adept at explaining the subtleties of their thought.

Any attempt to explain culture should use appropriate language that others can understand. The MIT researchers, for instance, did a masterful job introducing Toyota's *sogiotoshi* principle of removing excess and minimizing waste. So did the authors of *The Knowledge Creating Company*, Nonaka and Takeuchi, in their study of Japanese approaches to innovation and knowledge creation. I hope that many others will join this effort to share what is distinct about Japanese culture in a language that is accessible to all.

APPRECIATING JAPAN'S UNKNOWN INNOVATION

To share Japan's cultural DNA with the world, one must also learn to appreciate Japanese innovation and find imaginative ways of putting it to use. In 2012, the news that Professor Shinya Yamanaka of Kyoto University won the Nobel Prize in Physiology or Medicine for his work on induced pluripotent stem cells (iPS) was received with enthusiasm by the Japanese public. However, there is a great deal of innovation that still lies dormant and unknown.

Recently, I happened across a small newspaper column on the ucode system, a technical standard developed by YRP Ubiquitous Networking Laboratory (UNL) under the leadership of Professor Ken Sakamura of the University of Tokyo. The ucode system had been approved by the International Telecommunication Union – Telecommunication Standardization Sector (ITU-T). Impressed, I shared the news with several clients, only to receive lukewarm responses. When I asked a major distributor whether they would consider introducing ucode in their company, I was dismissed lightly with the remark that the ucode system was too costly and time-consuming to warrant implementing.

Likewise, the Japanese public showed little interest in the news that Hitachi's Cambridge Laboratory was collaborating with four other universities around the world to develop a new transistor that required no electric current to process information. I was even more astonished when I visited Hitachi and asked about the transistor, only to find that no one there knew anything about its existence. While the Japanese have good reason to celebrate the victories of their national women's soccer team, they also need to recognize the strengths of Japanese technology. The public's interest and support can make a huge difference. Once we start thinking of the world market as one great playing field, it becomes natural to respond with praise and excitement to the achievements of our fellow Japanese, no matter where in the world they might occur.

A NEW BUSINESS MODEL THAT CAN MAKE A DIFFERENCE

The third step in mobilizing the potential of Japanese cultural DNA - using it to design business models that make positive contributions to the world - is also the final stage. It would be a great satisfaction to see a "next generation model," capable of changing the ways of life of people around the world, emerge from Japan. In the past two decades, most influential next generation models and global standards have originated from the US and Europe. However, at a time when the knowledge industries have entered the mainstream, it is easier than ever to gather relevant data from a broad range of sources, extract useful information and provide added value, thereby producing new intelligence. The ability to create new models and future generation models is now within anyone's reach.

Many rich and unique features are enfolded into the Japanese cultural DNA. Finding ways to build creatively on their potentialities will be essential to creating new business models of Japanese origin. However, the Japanese cultural DNA seems to contain few "global" genes. The figure on the next page represents a schematic comparison of American, Japanese and Chinese cultural DNA. It suggests that the American cultural DNA is particularly suited for generating shared rules. The configuration of the Chinese cultural DNA is conducive to strategic thinking on large temporal and spatial scales. Coded in the Japanese DNA configuration is a disposition *monozukuri*. This is a skill the Japanese should self-consciously cultivate.

Comparison of Cultural DNA: US, Japan, and China

(CF) US	Japan	(CF) China
Protestantism	Shinto / agricultural theory of Japanese origins God = spirit	Confucianism and Taoism/ Horse-rider, nomadic theory of Japanese origins
• Freedom and equality of all human beings • Emphasis on rules and contracts • Democracy and the market principle • Human rights and humanitarian principles	• Endowing inanimate artifacts with soul • The "customer is god" principle • Importance of the actual site where business processes take place • Picking up on cues (non-verbal understanding) • One collective mind	• Conflicting and complementary aspects of Yin and Yang • Strategic thinking involving large spatial and temporal scales • The importance of seizing opportunities
• Aversion to frameworks and enclosures • Indifference to detail as long as the broad outline fulfills expectations	• Dislike of strategy and negotiation • Frameworks/enclosures • Attention to detail • Cooperation (exchange of favors)	• Aversion to frameworks and enclosures • Cooperation (exchange of favors)
• Linear narrative of progress (past → present → future) • Symmetry • Specialized knowledge and know-how + English + model construction → virtual teams	• Letting bygones be bygones; focusing on the future • Trimming away excess	• Using lessons from the past to prepare for the future • Diversity and nuance
C>F	C=F	C≈F

Notes: C>F Cultures where content is more important than form
C=F Cultures where content and form are integrated
C~F Cultures were content and form are equally important

CHAPTER 9
A LEARNING APPROACH FOR THE TWENTY-FIRST CENTURY (THE FIFTH PATH)
Becoming a Top-level International Player

THE FOUR STEPS OF A LEARNING APPROACH FOR THE TWENTY-FIRST CENTURY

To successfully navigate the global era, one has to confront the world as a whole, responding to all situations in a timely manner and seeking solutions to problems without first labeling them impossible. Success is, in other words, a matter of tapping into the largest possible market while at the same time mastering speed.

Traditional approaches to learning, which used to rely on the accumulation of fragmentary knowledge, are becoming increasingly obsolete. In this final chapter, we will consider what the transition to a twenty-first century approach to learning might entail. Simply put, the approach is a methodology for internalizing the global model introduced in this book, and using it to apprehend and construct one's own mental world in novel ways. Since this learning approach employs thought patterns and skills derived from the Eastern intellectual tradition, the Japanese will find it easy to relate to.

Why change established learning approaches in the first place? The urgency of the need for change became clear to me at the turn of the millennium, as major management associations and prominent business schools around the world were beginning to enter the field of global business training – a field I helped pioneer during my years in the US. How could I possibly compete with these rivals, who were armed with oodles of capital and talent? I had little chance of successfully opposing such powerful competitors by falling back on conventional learning methods. I brooded day and night over this situation, which occupied my every waking thought.

Until, after days and nights of wrestling with the problem, the idea of drawing on the resources of Eastern thought – from Zen Buddhist meditation to the idea of the "Way" (*michi*) – suddenly occurred to me. Amusingly enough, I even found myself contemplating the image of the twelfth-century warrior monk Benkei, with his legendary arsenal of seven weapons strapped to his back. To be among the winners of the global era, we must expand the capacity of our mind, using the principles of concentration and selection to amass knowledge, information, and experiential insight, so that they are immediately available when the need arises. Such an approach to learning, inspired by Eastern thought, is precisely what is most needed today.

Then, memories of professors I had worked with at the MIT Sloan School of Management and Thunderbird School of Global Management came to mind. These leaders at the forefront of the intellectual community must have been facing the same challenges that I was dealing with. And they were not the only ones. People everywhere were experiencing the effects of globalization, and seeking ways to develop the strength needed to survive these uncertain times. I felt that I, as a Japanese, could contribute to outlining a new approach to learning. I would start by enacting that change in my own life. With a newfound determination, I tossed the copies of my long-cherished marketing tool – my interview in TIME Magazine – into the wastebasket as I embarked on the next stage in my life.

CHAPTER 9 A LEARNING APPROACH FOR THE TWENTY-FIRST CENTURY (THE FIFTH PATH)

To better appreciate what the new approach to learning can offer, let us break it down into four steps.

Step One

Imagine your mind enveloping the globe. As you make space for the entire world to dwell in your mind, use both your physical eyes and your mind's eye to observe it. With physical eyes alone it is impossible to embrace the world in its entirety. We need the mind's eye to see what would otherwise remain invisible. The vast, swiftly changing world is beyond the reach of the physical eyes. To respond promptly to the problems you encounter, to acquire wisdom, and to glimpse into what the future holds, one must learn to see with the mind's eye. Are you ready to take a bird's eye view of the world in your mind with eyes wide open, should the need arise?

However, the notion of a mind's eye can be difficult to accept for some, particularly for Americans. I once gave a cross-cultural seminar for non-Japanese executive staff at the New York subsidiary of a well-known Japanese brokerage firm. At one point, I asked participants to assemble a virtual image of the world as a whole in their minds. One Latino staff member responded that he found such "esoteric, cult-like jargon hard to stomach."

In yet another instance, I was explaining the Japanese concept *of monozukuri* and its relationship with stringent quality expectations in manufacturing to the staff of an American company. As mentioned in a previous chapter, I referred to Shinto to emphasize the point that for the Japanese *monozukuri* is much more than science and technology. Central to the notion of *monozukuri* is the idea of a creator infusing one's spirit into the object to create an exquisite product. I was met with bewildered expressions. Sometimes, explanation is not enough to gain understanding. On the flip side, it is precisely these skills that defy easy explanation that can give the Japanese a significant advantage.

Step Two
Once you have a bird's eye view of the world you have assembled in your mind, spread out the Cultural World Map at its base, so that it remains clearly visible underneath all the layers. When working in the global market, you will often have to make decisions without all the facts in hand. At such times, even though you may intend to act as strategically and tactically as possible, ultimately you will need to rely on intuition. That is when having a visual representation of value systems at hand can be helpful, reminding you of the sometimes divergent ways of thinking with which Legal Code societies such as the US and Moral Code societies such as Japan operate.

The future of business is increasingly shaped by individuals with diverse cultural backgrounds cooperating with one another in heterogeneous teams. In many of these "global virtual teams" email is the primary means of communication. Members meet in person only once during the project – sometimes they never meet at all. A mental map is a valuable resource to turn to for reference when interacting with others in a global virtual team environment. Particularly useful tools include a membership chart (showing contact information, cultural code, time-zone difference, etc.), a chart of national holidays, religious celebrations and vacations, and a list of basic communication rules. Each of these tools can be used on a regular basis to facilitate communication with other team members.

Whether it be teleconferences or face-to-face negotiations, these charts will provide hints the instant you know what cultural region or country other participants come from. For example, you will have a better idea of what presentations will be effective, or what you should refrain from saying. Throw in the latest figures from your field of expertise, and your audience will quickly acknowledge your competence and professionalism.

In addition, the Cultural World Map encompasses histories of hundreds and thousands of years along the time axes under each of the four cultural codes. These axes of time and space will help you to not only communicate effectively with others, but also to process whatever relevant information you come across. For instance, referring to the axes of time and space will provide clarity when you explain a situation or report information via email in English to team members from a different cultural background. Using the two these axes will help you to correctly understand content from seminars and readings, and to organize the newly learned information, using matrix thinking to store it in the proper section of the mental map. This will enable you to integrate information on a wide range of issues, from Copernicus, to Confucianism, and to episodes from Japan's Edo period (1603-1867). As you become more adept at using new information as a building block in the construction of your own mental world, you will start to experience learning as a source of joy.

Step Three

If you work in business, your business world will be part of the mental map that you construct. By including not just the departments that are of direct relevance to your work, but your company's entire history and all of its current world market projects in the map, you will become able to detect the overall picture of the company's operations and trends from the same vantage point as the company's president or CEO. Of course, at the same time you will keep an eye on international competition. If, in addition, you provide advice that is beneficial to the company and put your best effort into your work, you will eventually position yourself as an outstanding candidate for an executive position.

Students, on the other hand, will find that a mental map affords them the ability to travel freely between the spatial representation of the world and a temporal axis spanning thousands of years. As they learn about world religions, compare Eastern and Western philosophies, or read the classics either in a formal classroom setting or through independent study, they can become well versed in the liberal arts. Keep in mind that a broad-based liberal arts education can ensure an effective leading edge in a global business environment.

Step Four

Subscribe to two paper-based daily newspapers covering world news and create scrapbooks with sections for the seven major world regions, as well as for individual countries, industries, companies, or whatever grouping works for you. Add important events and insights from your scrapbook to your mental world. You will find yourself slowly digesting the collection of news that shapes your inner world, with the latest and most important news continually bubbling to the surface. As the contours of your mental world come to be more clearly delineated, the initially laborious work of scrapbooking gradually becomes easier. Reading world-class journals is another great way to keep up to date on current events, but if you lack the time or energy to do so, stick to the summaries of journal articles published in daily newspapers. For further details on scrapbooking, refer to the earlier section in this book.

Try following these four steps for six months, observing the results. You'll be amazed at how your own mental world expands. This will help you develop the skills to pose meaningful questions and construct convincing arguments at the drop of a hat no matter who your audience is.

The fact that the Japanese have difficulty communicating their opinions to an international audience has been attributed to their insufficient English proficiency. This is not entirely true. Instead, I would argue that what the Japanese lack is a range of knowledge required for understanding the world. There is no doubt that English is much more than a means to a goal. Yet the real reason why the Japanese struggle with articulating their opinions is to be found not in the absence of content, but in its fragmentary character. In other words, their mental world has yet to take shape.

Now that we have looked at the foundations of a new approach to learning, we can proceed to an examination of what should be learned.

THE MINDSETS OF PREDOMINANT ETHNIC GROUPS

Let us assume that you have assembled a map of the world as a whole in your mind, and secured it firmly in place as the interpretive basis for your interactions and encounters. The next step is to identify the world's prominent ethnic groups and develop an overall understanding of their mindsets, as they emerge from a scrutiny of their past and present patterns of behavior. If we look around at the events happening in the world today, it is obvious that they are shaped by the historical trajectories of the particular ethnic groups involved. Today's headlines cannot be understood without a clear picture of their historical background. Learning history is one easy way to bridge between past and current events, but it should be accompanied by an effort to integrate national history into world history. The Japanese still tend to separate the two, making it impossible to see how Japanese history fits into a larger historical pattern.

But what does learning about people's mindsets involve? Let us proceed by way of an example and consider the Chinese mindset.

THE CHINESE (HAN) MINDSET

- Goal orientation

The table on page 174 compares the mindsets of three ethnic groups representative of the Confucian culture area. A distinct behavioral pattern that the Chinese seem to display as an ethnic group is their collective ability to set national goals and achieve them no matter what the cost. Since this behavioral pattern is driven to some extent by Sinocentrism (the traditional idea that China is the center of civilization and that other countries are on the periphery), it is ultimately connected to ambitions of establishing China's world hegemony. My point is not that companies should avoid doing business with China. Rather, I wish to draw attention to the existence of an ingrained Chinese mindset. The Japanese (yes, that includes me) tend to accept others in good faith and quickly trust them. Before doing so, though, it is important to familiarize oneself with the features of the Chinese ethnic mindset in order to promote fair business practices.

- Reluctance to allow foreign businesses to profit in the Chinese market (only Chinese businesses should profit)

At first, foreign companies bringing in capital and advanced technology are ardently welcomed in China. Once they start to make a profit, however, the communist psychology, which pits people against each other as "exploiters" and "exploited," rears its ugly head. In the past, this has led to boycotts of the factories of foreign owned corporations, anti-Japan riots, and frequent arbitrary changes in government policies and rules.

- A sense of time characterized by the application of past lessons to the future

The Japanese sense of time has traditionally been grounded in the notion of transmigration. Being based on the circularity of cycles of retribution, it allows you to let go of past errors and start afresh. In contrast, the Chinese do not forget the lessons of the past, but rather build upon them as they move into the future. Koreans do the same. This is why past Japanese invasions will never cease to be a sore subject. If you fail to realize this, you risk running into a plethora of unanticipated problems. It has now been more than two decades since I first traveled China's inland region. As I was preparing to my trip, an American specialist on China advised that I study modern and contemporary Chinese history before setting out. At the time I was not too concerned about history, but realized afterwards just how valuable this advice was.

- Speculative flair and a money-driven mentality

The Chinese are so adept in business that it seems inscribed in their genes. They also tend to focus more on individual rather than corporate profit in their transactions. At times, they will take short-term action to reap rewards, disregarding the principles of diplomacy and long-term trust.

- The importance of "face"

The importance of "face" (*mentsu*) is a common trait found in Moral and Religious Code countries. Those from Legal Code countries often have a hard time understanding why concerns with face should be dragged into the professional world. The Chinese have a particular sensitivity to face. For example, pointing out mistakes to a Chinese person can be inefficient and counterproductive, since they find it hard to accept criticism objectively and calmly, and may lash out in response. When the Chinese believe their honor has been compromised, they often resort to means of revenge.

- Use of opportunism to achieve their ends

The Chinese do not let opportunities slip by.

- Modes of thinking that use large-scale time and space axes

They are particularly skilled at thinking on a large scale: they see the universe as the product of the interacting polar forces of *yin* and *yang* and measure history in thousand-year units.

- A preference for solving problems behind closed doors

Decision-making processes are not made public.

- The principle of retaliation: if slapped in the face, slap back twice.

While the principle of retaliation is adhered to in various places around the world, it is particularly potent in Chinese society.

By examining, even cursorily, the multiple facets of a prominent ethnic group's mindset, we can become more discerning in our cross-cultural interactions. Thus, one lesson we can draw from the Chinese case is that, even though bilateral relations between Japan and China may improve in the years ahead, it is still prudent not to be overly trusting. Learn about the mindsets of another ten or so prominent ethnic groups, and you will find yourself equipped with an expanded understanding of the world.

Chinese, Japanese, and Koreans

(a) Chinese	(b) Japanese	(c) Koreans
• Strong goal orientation • Mobilization of all available means to pursue goals • Ease in letting go of established frameworks, as long as it facilitates goal achievement	• Frameworks perceived as powerful cultural motivators; strong management orientation • Flexibility as long as frameworks collapse or are not yet fully established • Compliance with frameworks that are already in place	• Frameworks perceived as cultural demotivators (triggers of resistance) • Liberation from frameworks perceived as an energizing cultural motivator
Continent	Island	Peninsula

THE TRICK TO LEARNING ENGLISH AND OTHER FOREIGN LANGUAGES

As I have mentioned several times in this book, one cannot become a global business professional simply by learning English. That being said, learning English is important. And still, there appears to be ample room for improvement when it comes to the learning methods used in Japan. Many methods emphasize short-term intensive language immersion in a classroom setting. A more effective approach, however, is to engage with the world as a whole in the process of learning. In other words, you need to get out there into the world, and take advantage of the richness that dialogue with others brings to language learning. Just as babies learn to speak by interacting with their mothers, this communicative approach can benefit foreign language learners. I know for me personally, my English improved the most when I had to respond to questions and engage in dialogues during my seminars and lectures. Having to pick up on the intent of each participant's question and provide immediate, professional answers worked wonders in polishing my English skills.

The same goes for writing. Emails are sites of struggle where you have to use English to persuade someone without actually meeting them face-to-face. I spent a fair amount of time mulling over how to craft my emails to entice potential customers. At times these emails would haunt me in my sleep, and I would wake up wondering if I had actually sent those messages off or not.

To learn English, the Japanese first complete a language training program, followed by travelling overseas. It is, however, too late. The logic behind this approach to language learning is similar to the one underlying decisions to venture overseas only after domestic demand has declined. Such approaches to learning and business have not come to terms with the needs of the global age – it now makes more sense to get out there and start interacting with others right away.

Learning how to explain your country's legal system in English is another way to not only improve your language proficiency, but also to cultivate a global mind. There is a huge demand for people who can explain Japanese laws in simple English to individuals from Legal Code societies who come to work in Japan. Brushing up on your knowledge of Japanese law will also help you develop your legal mind. For instance, you may want to be able to give explanations about:

- The Japanese Constitution (how it differs from your interlocutor's constitution; the problems it poses; etc.)
- Commercial law and other sections of the Japanese Compendium of Laws (*Roppo Zensho*) relevant to your interlocutor's business
- Japanese corporate rules
- Rules concerning everyday life in Japan
- Customary rules

Being able to talk about any one of these rules and laws in English will greatly work in your favor. There is no hiding from the fact that the Japanese need English to communicate at the international level. If you are going to invest the time, effort, and money in learning English, then you owe it to yourself to choose methods that will enrich your global awareness as well.

HOW TO TRAIN YOUR BRAIN TO CREATE NEXT GENERATION MODELS

There is one final skill I fervently wish to see the Japanese acquire: the ability to create next generation models. I have led training programs on how to start and develop global ventures, tailored to meet the needs of audiences in various regions of the world. I realized during these training programs that, whenever participants brainstormed about the businesses they wanted to establish, it was the Americans rather than Japanese that offered the most intriguing ideas. Such creativity should not be taken as evidence of an innate intelligence. Rather, it is nurtured by certain types of education and the availability of role models in close proximity. Japan has its own innovative business models, including Toyota's Kanban (a logistical chain control system) and lean production system (TPS), or Yamato Transport's door-to-door delivery service developed by the company's former president, Masao Ogura 37 years ago. However, lately innovation in new business models is staggering.

Consider the following examples. "Cloud computing" is an internet-based computing model born in Silicon Valley. Many believe that the concept of "cloud" became established after former Google CEO Eric Schmidt introduced it at an industry conference. The "smart grid" was developed and named by electric power providers in the US as part of efforts to modernize the energy sector. Not only the Silicon Valley, but the US and European economies more broadly continue to push innovative business models into the marketplace. So why is the situation different in Japan? The scarcity of role models in the immediate environment may be an important factor influencing the pace of Japanese innovation.

There is no need to be pessimistic though. Other recent developments offer reason for hope. Noteworthy is the spread throughout the world of microcredit, a model of social business initially created by Muhammad Yunus, the founder of Grameen Bank, to provide small loans to impoverished borrowers in Bangladesh. Another example is KidZania, a chain of theme parks designed to give children the opportunity to learn about adult occupations through role play in a replica city. KidZania was created by Mexican entrepreneur Xavier Lopez Ancona, who opened the first theme park in 1999 in

Mexico City. Since then, these theme parks have swept the overseas market like wildfire.

These examples prove that new business models do not need to originate in the Euro-American arena to succeed. With so much to offer, I am hopeful that innovators in Japan will start taking steps to forge original business models. These steps should include:

1) Becoming your own "think tank"

To become your own think tank, you need to work hard to obtain real-time information, particularly the kind of information that is making a transformative impact on the world. Pay attention when new, breakthrough models are announced and make an effort to understand how they were created. By researching and advocating new models and ideas you will build your think tank capability.

2) Using other models for inspiration

Merely imitating other models will not take you far. The Japanese love models and case studies, but tend to be lackadaisical when it comes to building off those ideas. It is important to remember that examining case studies is not an end in itself, but a starting point. Pick a few related case studies to see if you can identify common trends. See if you can make any eye-opening discoveries or dig deeper to identify tools that can be applied more generally to the analysis of other models. Take time to think through your material and see what creative uses you can put it to.

3) Using diagrams to make your explanations easier to understand

I have already touched upon the ingenuity of the Japanese when it comes to using diagrams and other visuals. The strategic use of diagrams to explain business models to foreigners has the additional advantage of minimizing the need for detailed explanations in English.

4) Putting your subconscious to work

Challenge yourself to constantly ask big questions: what sort of innovation would advance convenience for people everywhere? and what would assist those in disadvantaged environments? Let these ideals sink into your subconscious. Once they are firmly planted, you will find yourself naturally searching for new solutions. You will discover hints in books on seemingly unrelated topics, and ideas will come to you in your sleep.

5) Doing research on naming

Research the names of models used at the global level in various fields. Find words that can be used without requiring translation, expressions that appeal to the right brain, novel ways of using well-known terms, etc.

Finally, as I have emphasized throughout this book, it is important to command a view of the world you have assembled in your mind. Use a large-scale time axis to determine what the next stage should be, and what you need to accomplish. Not long after the turn of the millennium, Thomas Friedman pertinently noted that people's perceptions of the possibilities of globalization were changing around the world. Globalization, he wrote, was going to be increasingly driven by individuals who become empowered by adapting themselves to its processes.

In Japan, this transition has been slow. However, national crises such as the 2011 Great East Japan Earthquake and Tsunami or territorial disputes have served as a wake-up call, marking the beginning of a transformation in consciousness. If, at this point, Japan adopts a twenty-first century approach to learning and succeeds in developing global talent, it is positioned to establish itself as a top international player, possessing a distinctive identity that sets it apart from Europe and the US.

It is my great hope that Japan will retain this distinctive identity while at the same time evolving and absorbing new influences as globalization progresses. Only then will Japan be able to steer itself in the direction in which it can make its greatest contribution.

Conclusion

"Global" is the word on everyone's lips today, and yet few people live truly global lives. The main reason for this disconnect is that many fail to grasp the difference between "the world-as-a-whole" and "the world-as-overseas," mistaking one for the other. Before we start a discussion about how to develop global talent, we need to first reinvent ourselves as global individuals.

However, the information about the world that one can access in Japan tends to be fragmented and biased in nature. It takes creativity and effort to get an accurate picture of the world-as-a-whole. This book is intended as a resource for those who wish to gain a better understanding of the contemporary world.

Our discussion has covered a number of essential questions, including what form of globalization we should pursue, and how Japan's people and national strategies need to change for the nation to emerge as a key global player. But the central concern of this book is the need to reverse conventional learning methods on two levels.

First, stop conceiving of the world as an "overseas." Instead, frame your thinking with an awareness of the world-as-a-whole, and layer this frame with relevant and important content. The best time to cultivate a perspective that attends to the vast frame of the world-as-a-whole is now. Once you do so, it will also change your understanding of what counts as significant content.

Second, do not deal with the fragmented information that comes your way in a fragmented manner. Instead, construct a coherent mental world, rounding it out with details. Use both your physical eye and your mind's eye to observe the world as the occasion demands.

Organize the constantly incoming information on the two axes that structure your mental world. Then, use it as material for creating added value and new models.

Leaders whose work is making a global impact tend to share this kind of thinking. By mastering it, and complementing it with a commitment to maximizing scale, anyone can develop skills rivaling the greatest minds out there.

To this end, I recommend the following daily exercise. Have a broad vision that not only looks outward from within Japan, but also from the outside inward. Nurture a bird's eye view of the world as a whole. Then, focus on the balance between these three perspectives. It will soon make you realize

Japan's embeddedness in the Moral Code cultural region, where interpersonal relationships are perceived as primordial. If we treat life and business as if relationships were their sole axis, we risk missing much of what matters most. You may have had this experience: you sit in a bullet train looking out of the window, believing it is not you moving past the landscape, but the landscape leaving you. Likewise, while advocating the importance of developing global talent, you may remain loyal to moral code values as the only absolute standard, and reject the values and communication styles of other cultural codes. Oblivious of your own biases, you end up unwittingly undermining the very diversity you aim to foster, nipping global talent in the bud. This is why it is important to practice expanding your perspective on a daily basis.

Another effective exercise is to imagine humankind as one community of 7 billion people with no ethnic boundaries, in which each human life is equally precious. Use a horizontal rather than vertical logic to make sense of differences between self and other. Hold to this vision as you keep learning about historical and current events, organizing them along the axis of time, and committing them to memory.

Since the primary aim of this book is to contribute to a better understanding of globalization, we did not cover processes of localization, indispensable for moving global business projects forward, or the international model, which, despite no longer being the driving force of business, still retains its influence. While these are important elements, what it all comes down to is this: if you wish to reap the benefits of the global age, you need a clear grasp of the current state of the world, and of the direction in which humankind is headed, before you venture abroad. Travel overseas without this understanding, and you will soon find yourself caught up in the specifics of local situations, losing sight of the broad picture. The fastest way to grow as a global professional is to first develop a holistic perspective on the world.

Switching to the twenty-first century approach to learning described in this book may seem difficult at first, but the outcomes will be worth the effort. Making this switch is particularly crucial for those aspiring to take on a leadership role.

To conclude, I would like to express my gratitude to all who have helped and inspired me through the journey of writing this book. I am deeply thankful to Yoshiki Otake, founder and executive advisor of American Family Life Insurance Co. (AFLAC) Japan, for supporting me and believing in my work. Mr. Otake's strength and insight, his ability to overcome adversity and achieve success, have been a great source of encouragement to me.

I would also like to thank Hakubun Shimomura, whose lectures I have attended ever since we were introduced by Mr. Otake. Mr. Shimomura, who later became Minister of Education, Culture, Sports, Science and Technology, was the first politician that I found myself fully empathizing with. Japan is truly fortunate to have such talented and dedicated individuals, who work to further its global education.

Kentaro Yoshimura of PHP Institute was the finest editor I could have dreamed of. Having addressed some of Japan's faults in this book, it was no easy task finding an editor serious about publishing it. Mr. Yoshimura, however, took that work very seriously. Our respective strengths and expertise complemented each other superbly and made it a pleasure to work together.

I also wish to thank Hidemi Kawabe of Shinken Press, who introduced me to Mr. Yoshimura. The staff at Shinken Press and Yoshitsune Fujiwara provided helpful advice at the beginning stages of this book, and their support is deeply appreciated.

I also deeply thank Mandi Haase for translating and Laura Cocora, Ph.D, for editing the English version of the manuscript.

It has been an honor to work with so many inspiring and gifted people over these past five years. My heart is filled with a gratitude beyond words as I acknowledge the contribution of every person who made this project possible.

Thank you.

Glossary of Terms

This glossary provides basic definitions of the main terms used in this book, which may be unfamiliar to the reader.

International model vs. global model
- International: Relationships between countries.
- International model: A model focusing on relationships between countries.
- Global: Considering the world as one unit.
- Global model: A model considering the world as one unit.

Dualistic thinking vs. matrix thinking
- Dualistic thinking: Making binary choices between opposite values.
- Matrix thinking: Using two axes with opposite values to achieve total optimization.

Navigate (*kuguru*): The process of accumulating in-depth, embodied experience that aligns with the dual axes of space and time.

Liberal arts: Subjects or skills considered essential for global literacy; a basic understanding of world classic literature, religious philosophies, etc., as they are situated within the framework of large-scale spatial and temporal axes.

Ethics and morality
- Ethics: Universal principles that define virtuous conduct irrespective of time and place.

- Morality: Standards that define virtuous conduct relative to a specific time and place.

Cultural World Map and Global Navigator: Global business support tools developed by Ikuko Atsumi, which afford a general understanding of the mental patterns of the world's population of over seven billion people. These devices enable a quick grasp of the world, facilitating thinking on a global scale. When conducting global business and pursuing total optimization based on the axes of regulation and diversity, the Cultural World Map and Global Navigator serve to elucidate the diversity axis.

- Cultural World Map: A map dividing the world into four value systems based on the centers where values cluster – three cultural codes (Legal, Moral, and Religious Codes) and a mixed code variety in which at least two codes coexist (Mixed Code). Each code emerges along a temporal axis that reaches back to early Eastern thought (Confucianism) and the origins of the world religions.
- Global Navigator: The main component of the Cultural World Map. Includes notes on the traditions and values of 30 countries, classifying them into cultural motivators (factors that promote cohesiveness and incentivize local people), and cultural demotivators (factors that produce antagonism).

The three cultural codes and the Mixed Code: The Cultural World Map classifies the mental patterns of the world's population into three codes based on the specific centers where values tend to cluster. A code is the foundation of a society's norms. In Legal Code societies, values concentrate around regulation and knowledge. Moral Code societies emphasize hierarchy, and their values revolve around interpersonal relationships. In Religious Code societies, values cluster around divine teachings. Societies in the Islamic cultural region belong to the Religious Code because here God's teachings control all aspects of life. In Mixed Code societies, two or more cultural codes coexist side by side.

Cultural Motivators(SM) and Cultural Demotivators(SM)
    5)   Cultural motivators: Incentivizing cultural factors identified through the scrutiny of specific local cultures.
    6)   Cultural demotivators: Cultural factors that lead to antagonism.

Cross-cultural education and global education
- Cross-cultural education: Education that promotes understanding of different cultures and friendly relations among ethnic groups.

- Global education: Education that fosters an understanding of the integrated history of the world and humankind, and the capacity to search for solutions to existing problems and biases. Values strategic thinking, new humanitarianism, pacifism, and the creativity that emerges from the shared values of cultural DNA and liberal societies. Given its emphasis on translating these skills into contributions and changes of significance to the world as a whole, global education is integral to leadership education.

"The Way" or "Path" (Taoism; Japanese *dô, michi*) and "living globally": Taoism, a belief system indigenous to China, conceives of "the Way" as the cosmic, ultimate principle underlying the whole of creation. The Taoist goal of becoming one with the Way can be viewed as the Eastern version of "globalization." The concept of the Way has exerted a lasting influence on Japanese thought and life.

Brought about by massive changes in the contemporary world, globalization has a creative and productive dimension, affording opportunities to channel the globalized individual's energy and skills towards solving humankind's problems. However, while the Taoist ideal of becoming one with the Way shares certain similarities with the global vocation, their end goals are different.

A twenty-first-century approach to learning: Since both globalization and the philosophy of the Way are premised on the ideal of a globalized individual, the Japanese can draw on Eastern intellectual traditions, and in particular on the modes of thinking and practices associated with the Way, to construct their own "knowledge base," using it to respond to an ever-shifting reality and to train themselves as global business professionals.

This approach to learning, which matches the needs of the current global age, runs parallel with emerging developments in artificial intelligence using big data from digital networks.

Appendix

Global Navigator

- Historical Layers of Culture
- Cultural Motivators
- Cultural Demotivators

This section contains excerpts from the following case studies in the Global Navigator.

- Mainland China
- Singapore
- Indonesia
- Russia
- United States
- Brazil
- Japan

While these excerpts have been taken out of context and slightly modified from the original version in the Global Navigator, I hope that they will help provide insight into the specific history and values of each area presented. This section can be used as a guide in understanding the concepts discussed in this book.

Mainland China: Historical Layers of Culture

Western influence
- Open Door Policy (late 1970s)
- Transition from planned economy to market economy while maintaining communist rule

Communist ideology/ social structure (1949-1977)
- Large-scale social planning and ideological purification during the Great Leap Forward (1958-60) and the Cultural Revolution (1965)
- Secession of Taiwan
- People's Republic of China under Mao Zedong (1949)

Chinese Civil War

Foreign influence/ conflict (late 19th century-1949)
- The Sino-Japanese conflict and Japan's invasion of China
- Semi-colonial relations with Britain and other Western European countries

The first and second Sino-Japanese Wars

Boxer Rebellion

Buddhism and Taoism (2nd century AD)
- Customs that have influenced thought patterns and small/ family business practices
- Pursuit of spiritual truth
- Introduction of Buddhism from India, Persia and Central Asia
- Emergence of Taoism in China based on the ancient teaching of Lao Tzu

Confucianism (a 2500-year-long tradition)
- Profound influence on all aspects of life
- Situation-oriented
- Interdependence
- Orderly and hierarchical society
- System governing social behavior and ethics
- Developed from the teachings of the Chinese philosopher Confucius (around 500 BC)

Mainland China

Cultural Motivators for Mainland China

① **Monetary and personal incentives**
- Material compensation other than salary is a must. Payments and favors provided through personal channels are expected.

② **Power, authority, prestige**
- Important to make clear a company's status as indicated by its financing capabilities, technology rankings, etc.
- Position, financial power, status or family background function as effective indicators of prestige. Name-dropping is perceived as evidence of networking ability.

③ **Flexibility**
- The Chinese are very creative. Leave room for flexibility.

④ **Bargaining**
- Arguing about price is a constitutive part of everyday life.

⑤ **Showing deference**
- Take advantage of opportunities to emphasize your partner's strengths.

⑥ **Reciprocity**
- Guanxi (personal connections) are relationships structured by reciprocity. These connections are second only to the family in terms of importance.
- Favors (kindness, caring for others) extend beyond the framework of typical business and service, referring to the time, money, and effort one spends for the benefit of others. Caution is needed to avoid possibly illegal practices when adhering to the rigid principle of reciprocity.

⑦ **Cutting-edge technology**
- Interest in transfers of advanced technology is a strong incentive for working with overseas partners.
- Provide complimentary technical training when selling products.
- Follow-up technical service is expected as a matter of course.

⑧ **Symbolic expressions/hyperbole**
- Do not take ceremonial formulae and customary expressions at face value.
- When used in official meetings and at Chinese-style banquets, symbolic and hyperbolic language can be effective in building relationships.

⑨ **Holistic approach: start big, then zoom in**
- Officially prioritize national interest over corporate and personal interests.
- Establishing connections between your business and larger, more influential organizations or government agencies is advantageous. Facilitate understanding by starting with the big picture and then honing in on specific details when providing explanations.

⑩ **Closed-door deliberations / "off-the-record" methods of problem solving and conflict resolution**
- Accept apologies conveyed indirectly through actions.
- Allow for tensions and conflicts to be solved behind closed doors.

Note: Cultural Motivators (sm) 1, 2, 3, and 7 are common to mainland China, Hong Kong, Taiwan, Chinese communities in ASEAN countries, and Vietnam. 5 is a common trait of Moral and Religious Code societies. 6 applies to China, Korea, Japan, and many Latin American countries.

Mainland China

Cultural Demotivators for Mainland China

① **Criticism of China based on the assumed universality of the Legal Code.**
- Chinese political leaders and business people argue that criticism of China is inappropriate when premised on the alleged universality of human rights and free competition principles.

② **Loss of face**
- Loss of face is acutely felt, and will likely result in revenge.

③ **Direct criticism**
- No distinction is made between business know-how and private matters such as emotions.

④ **Not returning favors**
- Unreturned favors are viewed negatively and can result in loss of face.

⑤ **Lack of historical knowledge**
- Ignorance of history is distrusted.

⑥ **An excessively direct and open attitude**
- Being too direct or open can have a detrimental impact on relationships.

⑦ **Resistance to authority**
- General belief that one cannot defeat authority.

⑧ **Business-focused attitudes that disregard interpersonal relationships**
- Political interest and interpersonal relationships are major drivers of decision making. To strengthen relationships, take advantage of any invitations to social events.

⑨ **Rigid attitudes and ways of thinking**
- Aversion to being forced into fixed frameworks and to having to follow strict schedules, rules, regulations, ethical guidelines, etc.

⑩ **Indifference to hierarchy and protocol**
- Neglect of hierarchy and appropriate protocols will hinder business relations.

⑪ **Bowing too often or too deeply**
- The Chinese find bowing uncomfortable and embarrassing.

⑫ **Gifts unsuitable for personal use / Status-appropriate gifts**
- It is considered bad taste to offer expensive gifts to high-ranking individuals.

⑬ **Excessive individualism**
- China is a group-oriented society and excessive individualism is not tolerated.

⑭ **Lack of personal incentives**
- Failure to provide personal incentives will lead to loss of motivation.

⑮ **Seniority system**
- A seniority system, where salaries and benefits gradually increase with the length of employment, holds no appeal.

Singapore: Historical Layers of Culture

Singapore, Inc.
- Financial hub of Southeast Asia
- Gains formal independence as a sovereign city state (1965)

WWII

Indian influence (19th-20th centuries)
- Hindus, Muslims, Sikhs, Christians
- Increased immigration from India

Chinese influence
- Influence of Confucianism, Buddhism, Taoism
- Increased immigration from mainland China (early 1800s)

British/ European Influence (16th-19th centuries)
- Singapore grows into a flourishing maritime trade center under British rule
- Singapore becomes a British Crown Colony (1867)
- Portuguese trade, Dutch and British control of East Indies, establishment of Singapore as trading post for British East India Co. by Sir Stamford Raffles (1819)

1819: Founding of Modern Singapore

Islam
- Conversion to Islam by the founding ruler of Malacca sultanate, which includes Singapore (beginning of 15th century)

Malay rule
- Continuous control of the region by Southeast Asian sultanates
- Early settlement of Malay and Chinese migrants

Crossroads of cultures
- Outpost for Chinese, Thai, Javanese, Malay, Indian, and Arab traders

 # Cultural Motivators for Singapore

Note: Singapore's population is ethnically mixed, including Chinese (74%), Malays (13%), and Indians (9%).

① **Power, authority, prestige**
- Singapore is often described as a meritocratic society. Status is determined based on individual abilities, achievements and education, rather than considerations of race, religion, or family background. Brand names are regarded as status symbols.

② **System-oriented**
- Proficient in using systems to achieve expected results. Both appearance and content are considered important.

③ **Data**
- Preference for quantitative data. Tendency to rely on large amounts of data. Proposals lacking sound statistical information are often met with distrust.

④ **Educational credentials/ high salary (medical benefits included)**
- Singapore's education system is one of most rigorous in the world. Children's abilities are assessed early on through tests that place them into programs deemed suitable for their needs. This early classification determines their future educational and professional careers. Accordingly, pressure and competition are fierce.
- Professionals who have graduated from top-ranking universities are considered "elite". Job-hopping is common in the private sector, with mobility both within and between industries. Careful consideration is given to career-related decisions.

⑤ **Transparency**
- According to global corruption surveys, Singapore has been deemed one of the least corrupt countries in the world. Government officials and other high-ranking decision-makers are averse to using connections to request and grant "special favors."

⑥ **Seizing opportunities**
- Singapore is a hub for Asian businesses, and opportunities tend to come and go quickly. The need to make the most of the moment is therefore a strong motivator.

⑦ **A message-centered communication style**
- Singaporeans appreciate direct, straightforward communication and tend to be assertive in public settings and in interactions with the media. Participatory debates are possible.

⑧ **Cutting-edge technology and human resources**
- Efforts to attract foreign technology and expertise.
- Along with Shanghai, Singapore is an Asian Mecca for worldwide talent.

⑨ **High regard for women**
- Compared to other Asian countries, Singaporean women are influential both in the family and in the workplace. Many women hold top positions in government and the private sector.
- Dual-income families are the norm.

 # Cultural Demotivators for Singapore

① **Criticism of the legalistic environment**
  ● Criticism of Singapore's legalistic environment provokes resentment.

② **Accusations of arrogance**
  ● Offended when accused of arrogance, especially by neighboring countries such as China or Malaysia.

③ **Contentious issues between Singapore and Malaysia**
  ● Since Singapore gained independence from Muslim-majority Malaysia, certain issues regarding relationships between the two countries have remained highly sensitive; such topics should be avoided.

④ **Loss of face and direct criticism**
  ● Open criticism in front of others is demotivating and upsetting.

⑤ **Children's education**
  ● Criticism and advice regarding the education of children is often met with irritation.

⑥ **No understanding of "kiasuism"**
  ● "Kiasuism" is a much talked-about concept that roughly translates as "fear of losing out." Non-Singaporeans need to learn to appreciate the importance of this trait for Singaporean social life.

⑦ **Frameworks**
  ● Frameworks (e.g. long-term plans, organizational charts, goals, etc.) are regarded as lacking dynamism. Expectations of long-term loyalty to one organization have a demotivating effect.

⑧ **Risk taking**
  ● Singaporeans are risk averse. Given that situations of uncertainty may result in broken promises, it is prudent to prepare for sudden changes.

⑨ **Failure to establish relationships of mutual support**
  ● Trusting relationships are developed through reciprocity and mutual support. Someone who fails to abide by this unspoken rule risks being judged as taking advantage of others to achieve his or her own ends.

⑩ **Overemphasis of logic**
  ● Singaporeans are generally realistic and have a stronger sense of time and urgency than other Asian nations. They see protracted discussions as wasteful. There is nothing to be gained by winning an argument on logical merit alone.

⑪ **Idealistic attitudes**
  ● Singaporeans are highly performance- and result-oriented. Attaching too much value to conceptual plans, ideals, and goals is considered unrealistic and a waste of time.

⑫ **Work with no financial and material rewards**
  ● Non-material incentives (e.g. building a better society, honorary advisory positions, etc.) are ineffective.

Indonesia: Historical Layers of Culture

Indonesian Independence

Civil War
- The Indonesian Revolution (1998) and the first direct presidential election (2004)

Indonesia-Malaysia Confrontation
- Separatist movements; secession of East Timor (1999)
- Suharto's anti-communist, authoritarian New Order regime; rise of Islam
- Sukarno: Guided Democracy and secular nationalism enshrined in Pancasila

---

1950: Proclamation of the establishment of the Republic of Indonesia

---

Dutch Colonization (1602-1949)

War of Independence
- War of Independence against the Netherlands (1945-1949); the Netherlands grants Indonesia sovereignty (1949)

WWII
- Japanese occupation during WWII; Dutch reclaiming of Indonesia following the war
- The British return Indonesia to the Netherlands as a colony under the direct rule of the Dutch King (1815)
- Dutch East India Company in charge of administration and trade of "Dutch East Indies" (Indonesia) (17th -18th centuries)

Islam (12th-15th centuries)
- Conversion to Islam of almost all areas excluding Bali
- Last prince of Srivijaya Empire converts to Islam and founds the Sultanate of Malacca (beginning of 15th century)
- Arab spice traders bring Islam to Indonesia

Hindu and Buddhist Kingdoms (~200 BC - beginning of 16th century)
- Majapahit Empire: the last Hindu kingdom (1293-beginning of 16th century)
- Srivijaya Empire: grows around a Buddhist kingdom of Sumatra
- Indian traders bring Hinduism and Buddhism to the Indonesian archipelago

Early Migrations and Malay Culture
- Migration of seafaring Austronesian peoples from mainland Asia via Taiwan to Malay peninsula and the Indonesian archipelago; ancestors of modern Malays (~1500-500 BC)
- Waves of ancient migration over tens of thousands of years

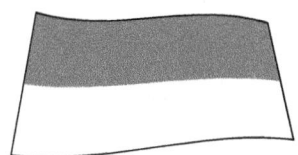 # Cultural Motivators for Indonesia

① **Belief in God**
- Islam is not the state religion. Indonesian Muslims tend to be moderate in their beliefs.
- Indonesia is governed according to the five principles of Pancasila: 1. belief in one almighty God, 2. national unity, 3. humanitarianism, 4. social justice, and 5. democracy. While religious freedom is guaranteed, faith is an important element of Indonesian life.

② **Building social networks (guanxi) through reciprocal relations**
- Ethnic Chinese, who make up 3% of Indonesia's population, control more than 80% of the country's private sector.
- Influenced by Confucianism, ethnic Chinese conduct business based on guanxi networks, which they develop through relations of reciprocity with both members of the Chinese community and local Indonesians.
- Many Indonesians learn business methods from ethnic Chinese.

③ **Hierarchical authority**
- Projects are implemented in top-down fashion. The motivation of individuals at all hierarchical levels is essential. Those at the bottom are errand runners.

④ **Self-control/ conflict avoidance**
- Direct confrontation is regarded as ill mannered. Controlled decorum, respect, and patience are key to getting things accomplished.

⑤ **Implicit formulation of opinions and criticism**
- In some situations, the intended meaning may be the opposite of that expressed by the words used. (This is especially common on certain islands. While this type of communication is not typical of all Indonesians, awareness that it exists can be helpful.)

⑥ **A correct understanding of Islam**
- Understanding of Islamic faith and tolerance towards other religions are important.
- While religion has, to a certain extent, an influence on business, cultivating amicable relationships with all cultural groups is more important.

⑦ **Diversity**
- There are many indigenous groups in Indonesia (Javanese, Balinese, etc.), each with its own unique culture. The Javanese are the largest ethnic group.

⑧ **Networking**
- Knowing the right people and having the right connections is essential for the collaborative relations that sustain joint ventures. It is customary to provide monetary compensation to intermediary agents. However, bribery is illegal.

⑨ **Being respectful of the observance of haram and halal**
- Haram refers to items and behaviors that are prohibited under Islamic law. Alcohol, gambling, and sensuous dancing and entertainment are considered haram. Halal refers to foods that Muslims are allowed to consume. Non-halal foods, such as pork and pork-based products, are not permitted.

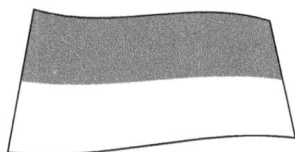
Cultural Demotivators for Indonesia

① **Insensitivity to what is considered sacred and taboo**
- Ignorance concerning sacred matters and religious taboos may act as a disincentive to potential Muslims and Hindu partners.
- It is insensitive to eat or drink in front of Muslims during the fasting month of Ramadan, to serve pork-based foods, or offer gifts made of pigskin. Women should cover themselves appropriately.
- Most Hindus are vegetarians. Cows are regarded as sacred.

② **Communication at face value**
- Indonesian communication is high context. Care should be taken not to embarrass others or cause them to lose face.
- Indonesians are reluctant to say "no" directly or discuss problems openly.
- Neither expect nor insist on straightforward communication. Many will agree just to avoid confrontation.
- Indonesians do not discuss their problems in front of others.

③ **Emphasis on punctuality, speed, and deadlines**
- Indonesians dislike being forced to prioritize efficiency over everything else. It is the norm for individuals in high positions to show up after everyone else has arrived. However, foreigners are expected to be punctual and efficient.

④ **Hurting national pride**
- Rampant corruption and separatist movements by ethnic groups (i.e. East Timor) are extremely sensitive issues.

⑤ **Causing others to lose face**
- Showing anger, pointing out mistakes, or criticizing someone in public will not only cause a person to lose face, but will negatively impact your image as well.

⑥ **Not returning favors**
- Indonesian business practices follow the Chinese reciprocity-based approach. Not returning favors is regarded as a form of injustice. Returning favors in a legally appropriate manner will help to build relationships of trust.

⑦ **Rude gestures**
- The following gestures are considered rude and/or vulgar: pointing at someone or something with your foot, pointing at someone with your index finger, showing the sole of your foot, standing with your hands on your hips, and slapping your right palm over your closed left fist.

⑧ **Unwillingness to learn the Indonesian language**
- Indonesians are very proud of their national language, and consider it a part of their cultural identity. Indonesians quickly lose interest in foreigners unwilling to learn the Indonesian language.

Russia: Historical Layers of Culture

Capitalism "Russian-style" (1991–present)
- Some acceptance of Western values
- Disintegration of egalitarian Soviet values
- Emerged in the 1990s in the wake of the perestroika reforms

Soviet Union (1922–1991)
- Collectivist ethos
- Egalitarian ideal
- Stability at the expense of change

WWII
WWI
Russian Revolution

Rise of Russian State (14th century – 1917)
- Dominance of the Russian Orthodox Church
- Aristocratic value system
- Rise of the tsars and birth of Russian empire
- Control over territory lost to Mongol hordes regained

Napoleon's invasion Russia

Asian influence
- Assimilation of Mongols and other Asian peoples into Russia
- Reflects Russia's unique position as a country straddling Asia and Europe
- Gained prominence following the Mongol invasions of the 13th century

Mongol invasion of Russia

Slavic paganism
- A deep undercurrent of pagan beliefs has influenced Russian life
- Folk superstitions, rituals, and celebrations
- Fatalistic inclination
- Migration of Slavic tribes from the 5th century AD

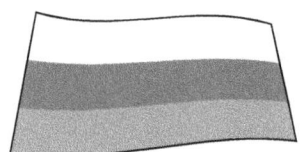 

Cultural Motivators for Russia

① **Influence and networks**
- Demonstrating influence is very important when doing business with Russians. High-ranking positions, titles, and other tangible signs of success such as expensive cars, large offices, etc. are effective ways to display influence.
- Influence is often expressed through networks – it is all about who you know and leveraging the right connections. Being able to enlist appropriate support is helpful for resolving issues promptly without having to reach for your wallet.

② **Respect for national traditions and achievements**
- Russians place a high value on their national achievements and traditions, reflecting perhaps an awareness of Russia's declining influence on the world stage. Patriotism is widespread among all age groups.

③ **Sincerity and genuine interest in others**
- Russians value sincerity.
- While politeness is important, excessive courtesy is regarded with suspicion. The ability to listen attentively and engage in lengthy conversations about personal matters demonstrates sincerity and a genuine interest in the other. While close relationships may take some time to build, once established they generally last a lifetime.

④ **Clear delineation of authority and responsibility**
- Russian society and organizations are hierarchal, with authority and responsibility clearly allocated at all levels. Make sure to correctly grasp the degree of authority and responsibility corresponding to each hierarchical level. Decision-making authority rests with those at the very top of an organization.

⑤ **Friendship-based networks**
- Russians attach great importance to friendships, especially those that are long-term.

⑥ **Duty towards relatives**
- Providing material support to relatives, particularly parents and siblings, is considered a duty.

⑦ **Important role of emotions and external factors in decision making**
- Decision-making is driven not by rational and analytical approaches, but rather by perceptions of what counts as appropriate, which are external to business itself: owners' or top management's personal preferences and beliefs, patriotic and nationalistic considerations, friendship and family connections, etc.

⑧ **Family-style relationships in the workplace**
- Paternalistic attitudes characterize relationships between bosses and subordinates in government, state-owned enterprises, and the private sector.

⑨ **Clear definition of gender roles**
- Traditional gender roles are still pervasive in Russia.

⑩ **Work-life balance**
- Russians do not "live to work." They expect all national holidays to be observed. A fast-paced, busy workplace can be highly stressful for Russians.

⑪ **Hospitality and treatment of guests**
- The Russian tradition places a high value on welcoming guests by opening for them the doors of one's home. Russians greatly appreciate hospitality, taking it as a sign that the host is interested in strengthening the relationship.

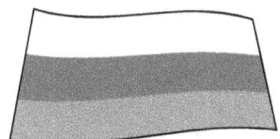 # Cultural Demotivators for Russia

① **Rigid adherence to rules and regulations**
- The notion that rules are arbitrary and do not have to be strictly adhered to is common among Russians, who routinely break rules in business and private life. People who play by the rules are considered naïve and unrealistic.

② **Standing out from the crowd and being too successful**
- Russians have ambivalent feelings about displays of success. Successful and wealthy individuals are the target of envy, while being at the same time perceived as dishonest.
- Bragging about one's success and aggressive self-promotion evoke a negative response from Russians.

③ **Excessive attention to detail**
- Russians prefer general outline agreements and verbal promises, leaving details to be hammered out later.

④ **Lack of social skills and a propensity for social isolation**
- Russians expect their colleagues and partners to socialize with them in informal situations both in and out of the office.

⑤ **Excessive caution and calculation**
- Excessively cautious people as seen as either cowardly or impudent.

⑥ **Criticism and condescension towards Russians and Russian ways of doing things**
- Russians are extremely sensitive to open criticism of Russians attitudes and ways of doing things, especially when it comes from foreigners.

⑦ **Relationships lacking an emotional and spiritual dimension**
- Russians consider emotional and, in some cases, spiritual aspects of relationships very important. Even in strictly business situations, they can become emotional and bring in personal elements. Emphasis on humanity and feelings rather than rationality is common. An "all-business, all-the-time" attitude is bound to create resentment.

⑧ **A widening gap between winners and losers**
- Russians have a strong egalitarian streak, and the majority of the population disapproves of the growing gap between the rich and poor. They expect the state to alleviate disparities in wealth, but are reluctant when it comes to paying taxes.
- Russians reject the type of inequalities embedded in the American socio-economic model.

⑨ **Disloyalty**
- Loyalty is the cornerstone of both business and personal relationships, and involves providing unconditional acceptance and support in all situations. The pursuit of self-interest at the expense of colleagues is abhorred and may result in severe denunciation, destroyed relationships, or ostracism.

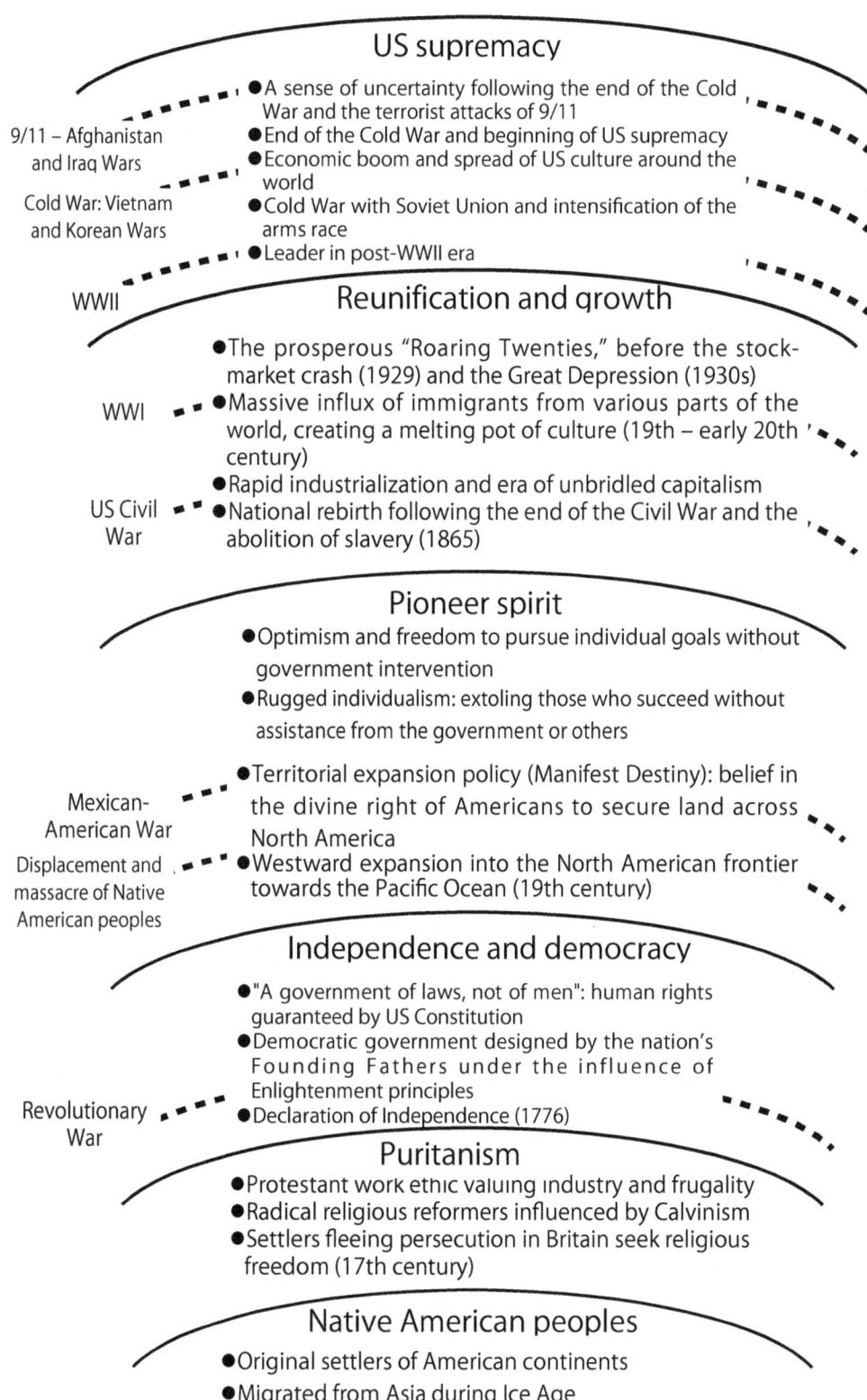

Cultural Motivators for the US

① **Checks and balances**
- One of the most important values in achieving free and fair competition. Corporate structure designed to separate policy makers (board members) from executors (CEOs, CFOs, etc.).

② **Professionalism**
- Work attitudes focused on efficiency in maximizing output within specific time constraints, while relying on expertise and minimizing personal considerations.

③ **Expertise/ career building**
- Expertise = education beyond a bachelor's degree + years of experience. Americans buy "expertise" (a highly individualized "product" that can be sold) to ensure prompt, positive results.
- Career development consists of constantly upgrading one's expertise so that it can be sold at a greater price.

④ **Responsibility = authority = remuneration**
- A basic formula commonly accepted and applied by business managers and employees.

⑤ **Bottom line**
- Net profit or loss, usually on a quarterly basis. The most important financial figure for enterprises.

⑥ **Accountability**
- Logical and professional disclosure of information pertaining to one's work and official duties.

⑦ **Prioritization**
- It is important to perform efficiently, achieving maximum results in a limited amount of time.

⑧ **Feedback**
- In American-style communication, feedback is essential for things to move forward.

⑨ **Fairness**
- Emphasizes equal opportunities, rather than equal results. A core value of free competition.
- Fairness in evaluation consists of setting fair and explicit criteria, applying those criteria fairly, and ensuring that results appear fair. Quantitative measurements are often used.

⑩ **Praise**
- Clear, verbal recognition and positive feedback boost motivation. Americans grow up used to receiving praise and expect it on a regular basis.

⑪ **Ownership (a strong sense of personal connection to one's work)**
- Ownership means taking responsibility for one's own decisions and actions and not blaming others for their effects.

⑫ **Contracts and privacy**
- Contracts must be honored under all circumstances.
- Privacy is one of the basic human rights guaranteed by the Constitution. Safeguards employed to protect privacy include numerous regulations and restrictions.

⑬ **Human rights, empowerment and diversity**
- he human rights guaranteed in the Constitution are considered fundamental values, underlying the entire legal order.
- Empowerment: enhancing the capabilities and power of those who are socially disadvantaged.
- Diversity: promoting diversity in the workforce and capitalizing on difference.

Cultural Demotivators for the US

① Impracticality
- Americans are skeptical of ideas and theories that appear to have no practical application. They tend to rely on empirical observation and measurement. Given that the US is a Legal Code society where values revolve around facts, Americans distrust conclusions based solely on ideas, unsupported by factual information.

② Hierarchy and formality
- Americans are unaccustomed to context-specific variations in hierarchical relations, and seek to establish equality. They dislike flowery rhetoric, convoluted speech, and excessive formality. Insistence on form and protocol is interpreted as pomposity and arrogance.

③ Silence
- Silence tends to be viewed as wasteful and awkward.

④ Seniority system
- For Americans, a seniority system is the equivalent of an anti-meritocracy. It has strong disincentivizing effects.

⑤ Name-dropping
- If overused, name-dropping can create an impression of frivolity.

⑥ Lack of personal space
- Physical space is important. Physical proximity is usually perceived as either threatening or having sexual implications.

⑦ Disproportionate use of intermediaries
- Relying on intermediaries to diffuse tensions and resolve problems is considered inefficient and dishonest.

⑧ Unclear distinction between public and private matters
- Americans expect a clearly delineated boundary between personal and work-related matters.

⑨ Unfamiliarity with the English language
- Fluency in English is highly valued as evidence of global competence.

⑩ Belief that humankind does not enjoy a special place in the order of creation (denial of creationism
- Some Americans are skeptical of cultures that see humans as just one life form among many.

⑪ All talk and no action
- Americans become restless when there are long periods of inactivity or lack of progress on a project. Results need to be personal, visible, and measurable. Americans insist on expressing their opinions and being given the chance to influence group decisions. Participation is a prerequisite for taking action.

⑫ False expectations about personal relationships
- Americans maintain numerous informal relationships, and enjoy the advantages of having a wide network of acquaintances. Gifts and invitations are appreciated, but there is no obligation to reciprocate. It is important to avoid anything that might be interpreted as an illegal bribe.

Brazil: Historical Layers of Culture

Contemporary Brazil
- Economic stability and growth
- End of dictatorship and transition to democratic government

Republic of Brazil
- Military regime marked by censorship, repression, stagnation, inflation and crisis (1964-1985)
- Populism and dictatorship (1930-1945)
- Economic growth, industrialization, and recruitment of immigrant labor from Germany and Italy under the "Old Republic" (1889-1930)
- Establishment of republican government (November 15, 1889)

Empire of Brazil (1822-1889)
- Abolition of slavery under Pedro II
- Establishment of the Brazilian monarchy
- Independence from Portugal (September 7, 1822)

African influence
- African religious beliefs combined with the beliefs of Brazil's indigenous peoples and Roman Catholicism give rise to so-called "hybrid religions" such as Candomble and Catimbo.
- Extensive intermixing between individuals of European and African descent
- Millions of slaves brought forcibly from Africa beginning in the 16th century

Portuguese colonization (1500-1822)
- Introduction of Roman Catholicism by Jesuit missionaries seeking to convert native populations
- Portuguese exploration and settlement of Brazil
- Arrival of Portuguese (1500)

Indigenous peoples
- Semi-nomadic tribes subsisting on hunting, fishing, gathering, and shifting cultivation
- Migrated from Asia during Ice Age

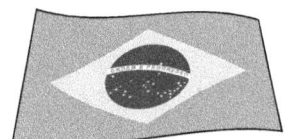 # Cultural Motivators for Brazil

① Dignity and respect
- Important to treat people as equals, especially in urban areas. Brazil is a people- and relationship-oriented society. More than half of Brazilians consider themselves to be of European descent.

② Personal connections
- Relationships play a decisive role in business. Introductions by trusted mutual acquaintances can make a difference in moving things forward.
- Do not jump right into business discussions. Find a topic of common interest to start a conversation, such as family, friends, etc.

③ First family, then business
- The family is the top priority. Be sure to ask about family; show interest and listen attentively when the subject is raised. Be prepared to talk about your own family.

④ Flexible sense of time
- Although Brazilians generally have a relaxed attitude towards punctuality, they expect foreign visitors to be on time. Being up to ten minutes late is not considered a violation of punctuality in Brazilian culture.

⑤ Emotional vs. rational
- It is important to separate business from private life. Brazilians tend to be indirect when it comes to discussing issues concerning personal relations.

⑥ More detail-focused than holistic
- Brazilians tend to start by examining the details specific to each situation.

⑦ Form over content
- Brazilians are rather formal at first, and tend to judge others based on appearance.
- Projecting an impression of professionalism is important (i.e. dress code, business cards, etc.)

⑧ Principle of reciprocity
- Brazilians are always courteous and expect the same from others.
- Sincere compliments about the country (i.e. nature, food, music) are appreciated.

⑨ Learning the ropes (= finding the right technique; taking shortcuts)
- Brazilians are creative at problem solving and believe there is always a way to accomplish the task before them.

⑩ Top-down decision making
- Decisions are typically made in the upper echelons of an organization.

⑪ Brazilian rhythm and food
- It is important to become accustomed to local rhythms and culture (Samba and other popular dance forms, regional varieties of Bahian fish stew, churrasco grilled meat, tropical fruits, Brazilian movies, etc.)

⑫ Soccer and carnival
- Always ask Brazilians about their favorite soccer team or club, and how it has been performing recently.
- Never schedule business prior to, during, or directly after the Carnival in Rio de Janeiro because no business takes place during the celebrations.

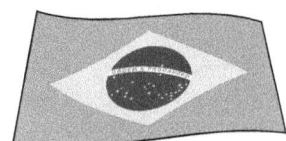

Cultural Demotivators for Brazil

① **Stereotyping**
- Although Brazil is world-renowned for its artful soccer and carnival extravaganza, it is important to be aware of the multiple facets of Brazilian life.
- Avoid patronizing or condescending attitudes.

② **Superiority and arrogance**
- Brazilians dislike being looked down upon. Most Brazilians are well-educated, can speak other languages, and have a good grasp of domestic and world affairs.
- Avoid comparing your own country and its culture to Brazil in a way that implies superiority.
- It is a common practice to address people by their title followed by their given name (i.e. Dr. Ricardo).

③ **Lack of knowledge**
- Lack of knowledge about other countries is interpreted as a sign of ignorance and lack of interest.
- Familiarize yourself with the Brazilian currency (Real), language (Portuguese) and national capital (Brasilia) when working with Brazilians.

④ **Imposing one's own business culture**
- Foreign business partners are expected to follow Brazilian business protocol. When negotiating with Brazilians, avoid trying to impose your own work pace.

⑤ **A "win-or-lose" approach**
- Brazilians dislike being taken advantage of. Avoid approaches that only benefit one of the parties; propose instead "win-win" initiatives.

⑥ **Deceitfulness**
- Relationships of trust take time to develop. Integrity is highly valued. Making big promises and not following through is considered deceitful. Lying and stretching the truth is not acceptable. Avoid double standards.

⑦ **Getting right to the point**
- Business interactions typically follow the same patterns as personal relationships.
- Attempting to immediately get down to business without first building a relationship may undermine your efforts. Financial issues (such as payment terms) and negotiation conditions are best discussed in the final stages of business dealings.
- Outlines and action plans can be effective in ensuring that everyone is on the same page. Specify roles, responsibilities, and timeframes.

⑧ **Lack of flexibility**
- Brazilians may react negatively to attempts by foreign business partners to impose their own rules.
- The Brazilian sense of time is elastic. Allow some flexibility in schedules and deadlines.

Japan: Historical Layers of Culture

Westernization (1868-present)

- High yen crisis, collapse of bubble economy, "lost decade"
- Miraculous economic recovery under the protection of the US
- Pacific War, defeat, and San Francisco Peace Treaty (1951)
- Japanese invasion of China and Russia, Manchurian Incident
- Meiii Restoration (1868) and embrace of Western culture

WWII

Secluded feudal state (1590-1867)

- Neo-Confucianism and bushidô (the "way of the warrior")
- Tokugawa shogunate and 260 years of isolation from the rest of the world
- Unification of Japan (1590)

Rise of the samurai (warrior) class (late 12th - late 16th century)

- Muromachi shogunate; rise in power of the common people
- Zen Buddhism (enlightenment through intense concentration of mind)
- Kamakura shogunate

Legislation-based state (7th century-1184)

- Shift from aristocratic Buddhist culture to a specifically Japanese culture
- "Imperial rescript" (ritsuryo) state modeled after the Chinese system (middle of 7th century)
- Buddhism (harmony) and Confucianism (emphasis on roles and duties) introduced from China
- Shinto (animistic, indigenous belief system); establishment of the imperial state

Antiquity

- Unification under the Yamato Court
- Beginning of rice cultivation (3rd century BC) and regional power disputes
- Trade with China as a vassal state
- Attunement to the laws of nature

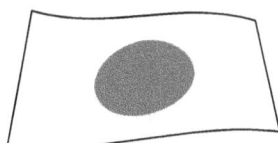 # Cultural Motivators for Japan

① Frameworks and enclosures
- The Japanese have a predilection for standardized organizational charts and long-term business plans. Employees carry out their jobs under detailed instructions and regular supervision, and frameworks are strictly adhered to. Having to work scrupulously within a framework brings out the most remarkable abilities of the Japanese.

② Quality (form = content; meticulousness)
- It is said that, "the Chinese are merchants by nature; the Japanese, craftsmen."
- High quality is one of the strongest motivators for the Japanese.
- The Japanese uphold a rare ideology that posits the equivalence of form and content. Packaging is part of a product. A good outer appearance is seen as a reflection of the quality of the content. Cosmetic flaws and dents are not acceptable. Similarly, a person's attitude is considered an expression of their character and abilities.

③ Genbutsu (actual objects) and genba (actual site)
- Under the influence of Shinto, which worships spirits dwelling in nature and things, the Japanese place high value on objects perceived to have a "soul." . On the flip side, abstract ideas, concepts and theory for theory's sake are demotivators.
- Verbal communication is more effective when associated with "actual objects" (a business card, token gift, information package, etc.). Such exchanges help strengthen relationships. Preparing drafts, blueprints, prototypes, and models that can serve as a basis for discussion will help work run smoothly.
- The Japanese find it difficult to evaluate a situation without visualizing the site as if they were actually there. For this reason, samples, models, and prototypes can serve as effective props.
- Actual business sites, such as manufacturing plants, are highly regarded as places where one gains practical experience and knowledge. It is advisable to include a visit to the genba when Japanese clients or prospective partners visit.

④ Standardized greetings; group greetings
- Proper greetings are essential for maintaining good relationships with the Japanese. A cheerful and positive tone of voice is important when greeting others. Initiating and ending interactions with adequate greetings will strengthen relationships and convey an impression of reliability.
- In building relationships, the most effective and frequently used formula is yoroshiku onegaishimasu, a phrase conveying appreciation for the other person's future cooperation and goodwill. The expression implies a desire to preserve a smooth relationship with one's interlocutor.
- Greetings on the occasion of personnel changes and reassignments ritually mark the transfer of responsibility from former staff to their successors.

⑤ The "client/customer is god" principle and total care service
- In Japan, the client enjoys a status higher than in any other country. This notion is aptly captured in the expression, "the client/customer is god." Clients are amicable as long as high-quality total care service is provided.
- Both quality and deadlines are of utmost importance. In the event of a major problem, a troubleshooter is dispatched to the client's site and an unqualified apology is expected (clients do not receive questionnaires asking them to identify the problem).
- Total care service means providing free service and demonstrating commitment to clients. If deadlines for rush orders need to be met, it is expected that staff will work weekends. Golf tournaments, lavish dinners and other annual functions are planned with the aim to please clients and maintain good relationships.

⑥ Unqualified apologies
- It is crucial to apologize immediately and wholeheartedly without making excuses. The moment you start analyzing the situation and giving explanations, this ritual loses its

effectiveness. An apology should be followed by an expression of regret and an offer to remedy the situation.

⑦ Exchange of favors and principle of reciprocity
- In Moral and Religious Code societies, reciprocal relationships based on exchanges of favors are essential for building relationships of trust.
- The principle of reciprocity is an unwritten rule. Failure to reciprocate and the accumulation of favor debt will end up damaging trust relationships.

⑧ Consensual decision making and participatory leadership
- Japan is the only Asian country that uses a consensus-based decision-making process (known as ringi).
- Senior executives who participate in activities on the same level with general staff are respected and popular within their organizations. Japanese executives do not hesitate to use the same parking lot and cafeteria as regular employees.

⑨ Japanese notion of sincerity (seijitsu)
- Seijitsu is a powerful formula for building trust. However, the English counterpart of the word, "sincerity," conveys different nuances, and at times even opposite meanings.
- In the case of seijitsu, the emphasis is on the selfless efforts one makes for the benefit of others. The term "sincerity," on the other hand, signifies consistency in word and deed. The Japanese work hard at expressing sincerity, but in many cases what they say does not match what they do. This is a reflection of such Japanese dichotomies as the one between tatemae (socially and politically correct behavior) and honne (true feelings), or between omote (the front) and ura (the back). To many non-Japanese, the Japanese appear to act according to double standards. Such conceptual differences have occasionally given rise to problems and bred distrust.

⑩ Holistic approaches
- The Japanese prefer to approach situation by grasping the overall picture first and then narrowing down the focus. In explanations and presentations, as well as when negotiating or creating promotional flyers, getting right to the point without first setting the context can complicate understanding for your Japanese partners.

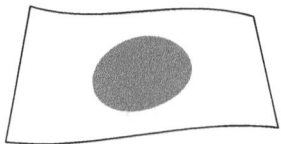

Cultural Demotivators for Japan

① Tenacious and contentious negotiations
- The Japanese particularly dislike contentious negotiations about money. Negotiating is perceived as an ignoble and impure activity. It is wiser to concede early on and be accepted as one of the "group", thus securing future lucrative opportunities.

② Poor customer service and arrogant vendors
- In Japan, customers are treated with the utmost respect. Those in retail and the service industry are expected to abide by the "customer is god" principle.

③ Not putting forth one's best efforts
- The amount of effort devoted to a task is an important criterion in the evaluation of a person's work.
- Actual results are secondary to the effort one is perceived to have put into their work.

④ Having to choose between two options (black or white/yes or no choices)
- The Japanese will often remain silent when forced to make a clear choice between two options.

⑤ Omission of greetings
- Failure to greet or return greetings will create a negative impression of arrogance, self-centeredness, or intention to cut off relations.

⑥ Carelessness
- Carelessness is unacceptable in both manufacturing and relationships.
- Failure to stay in touch, report and consult is seen as a sign of carelessness in communication.

⑦ Individualism and a self-centered attitude
- The Japanese perceive assertive individuals as self-centered.

⑧ Not returning favors and not expressing gratitude
- The Japanese are very meticulous in keeping track of exchanges of favors. They are careful to repay all favors, and expect others to do the same.

⑨ Argumentativeness
- Someone who relies on logical arguments to explain things or persuade others risks being regarded as a quibbler. Do not expect to be able to force your views on your Japanese partners by resorting to sophistry.

⑩ Lack of flexibility
- A person who refuses to bend over backwards to accommodate requests, or is unwilling to make adjustments to fit the situation is considered inflexible.

⑪ A bluntly legalistic attitude
- Since the Japanese do not have a strong legal mindset, a legalistic attitude can have destructive consequences on relationships of trust. Consulting with an attorney should be the last resort in resolving problems. A pledge (moral document) has binding force on the parties' actions.

References

Cultural World Map. Sekaichizu Co. Ltd. (Japanese version 2008, English version 2012).

Cultural World Map Reference Pamphlet. Sekaichizu Co. Ltd. (Japanese version 2009, English version 2012).

Global Navigator: A View of the Traditions, Cultural Motivators SM, and Cultural Demotivators SM of 30 Different Countries. Multicultural Playing Field, Ltd. (2007).

Hitachi IA Global Talent Development: eL Education for Promoting Global Mindset and Multicultural Understanding. Hitachi Information Academy Co., Ltd. (2012).

For more information on efforts in global education, please contact via the following:

http://www.ikukoatsumi.com
http://www.global-kyoiku-ken.jp/

Ikuko Atsumi

Ikuko Atsumi is the Director of the Institute for Global Education and President of Global Education Inc. After graduating from Aoyama Gakuin University graduate school in Tokyo, she was appointed as an assistant professor at her alma mater, and then went on to become a researcher at Harvard University. In 1983, Atsumi established a consultancy in cross-cultural management training in the suburbs of Boston - the first of its kind in the U.S. Her training program gained fame after being featured in TIME magazine, and the firm started providing personnel training and global market strategy solutions to numerous blue-chip U.S. corporations.

Atsumi's corporate clients have included top Fortune companies such as IBM, Ford, Xerox, and Bausch and Lomb. For 15 years, she was in charge of executive training at DuPont Worldwide and United Technologies. Many corporations have adopted the Cultural World Map developed by Atsumi as a basic tool for their global education programs. In 2001, Global Education Inc. entered the Asian market with the opening of its Singapore office.

Since returning to Japan in 2007, Atsumi has continued to provide global talent training programs for major Japanese companies, while also promoting global education for children. She currently serves as the Vice Chairman of the Education Subcommittee of the Japanese nonpartisan national policy think tank The National Vision Research Institute.

www.ingramcontent.com/pod-product-compliance
Lightning Source LLC
Chambersburg PA
CBHW080540170426
43195CB00016B/2627